JAMIE SMART'S

BUNNY VS MONKEY AND THE HUMAN INVASION!

Dedicated to all the amazing readers of The Phoenix!

The comics in this book were originally published as
Bunny vs Monkey: The Stench and *Bunny vs Monkey: The Wobbles.*

Adaptation and interior design by Laura Bentley, additional artwork and colours by Sammy Borras.
Cover design by Paul Duffield.

Bunny vs Monkey: The Human Invasion
is A DAVID FICKLING BOOK

First published in Great Britain in 2021 by
David Fickling Books,
31 Beaumont Street,
Oxford, OX1 2NP

978-1-78845-195-6
3 5 7 9 10 8 6 4

David Fickling Books reg. no. 8340307

A CIP catalogue record for this book
is available from the British Library.

Printed by Grafostil, Slovenia.

Papers used by David Fickling Books are from
well-managed forests and other responsible sources.

JAMIE SMART'S

BUNNY VS MONKEY AND THE HUMAN INVASION!

BUNNY
WEENIE
PIG
LE FOX

SKUNKY
MONKEY
METAL STEVE
ACTION BEAVER

"LOG OFF"

HEY, WEENIE! PIG! WOULD YOU HELP ME?

I'M GOING OUT TO LOOK FOR FIREWOOD.

HEE HEE! NOPE!

WE'RE HIDING!

HIDING? FROM WHAT?

WELL, I'M HIDING FROM PIG BECAUSE HE'S WEARING A **SCARY MASK!**

AND I'M HIDING FROM WEENIE BECAUSE HE'S WEARING A **SCARY MASK** TOO!

WELL, OKAY. I'LL GO AND FIND SOMEONE ELSE TO HELP ME.

SOMEONE LIKE... ACTION BEAVER!
WOOF!!

NOW, I NEED YOU TO HELP ME CHOP DOWN A FEW DEAD TREES, OKAY?
NOTHING CRAZY. DON'T FREAK OUT.
FFTTT...

...PING!
WHAT? WHAT IS THAT?
BOOM!
BOOP BOOP BOOP
BOOM!
BOOM!
NEEYOW!
AARGH! YOU ALREADY PLANTED EXPLOSIVES ON THE TREES?

YOU'RE INSANE! ALSO I CAN'T USE THESE, THEY'RE WET NOW.

HMM, HANG ON. ACTION BEAVER IS A BEAVER. SO HE MAKES DAMS OUT OF WOOD.
HE MUST HAVE SOME IN STORE.
PYIP! PYIP! PYIP!
OH, IT WOULD BE FAR EASIER IF YOU HAVE A FEW SPARE LOGS I COULD BORROW, ACTION BEAVER. I'D BE VERY GRATEFUL.
YARRRP! OW!
GOODNESS!
WHERE DID YOU GET ALL THIS WOOD FROM?
FSCHHH!
WELL, I CERTAINLY DON'T NEED THIS MUCH. PERHAPS I COULD JUST CHOP OFF A FEW BITS AND TAKE THEM BACK TO MY HOUSE...
HANG ON. DIDN'T I HAVE AN AXE WITH ME?
CHA-CHINGG!
NO, ACTION BEAVER. DON'T DO WHAT I THINK YOU'RE GOING TO DO...

CHING!
YAAAAARGH!!
RUMBLE!
RUMBLE!
RUMBLE!
NOT MY HOUSE!
NOT MY HOUSE!
CRASH!
AGAIN!
SIGHH. A COLD WINTER IT IS, THEN.
BOO!
BOO!
SCREAM!

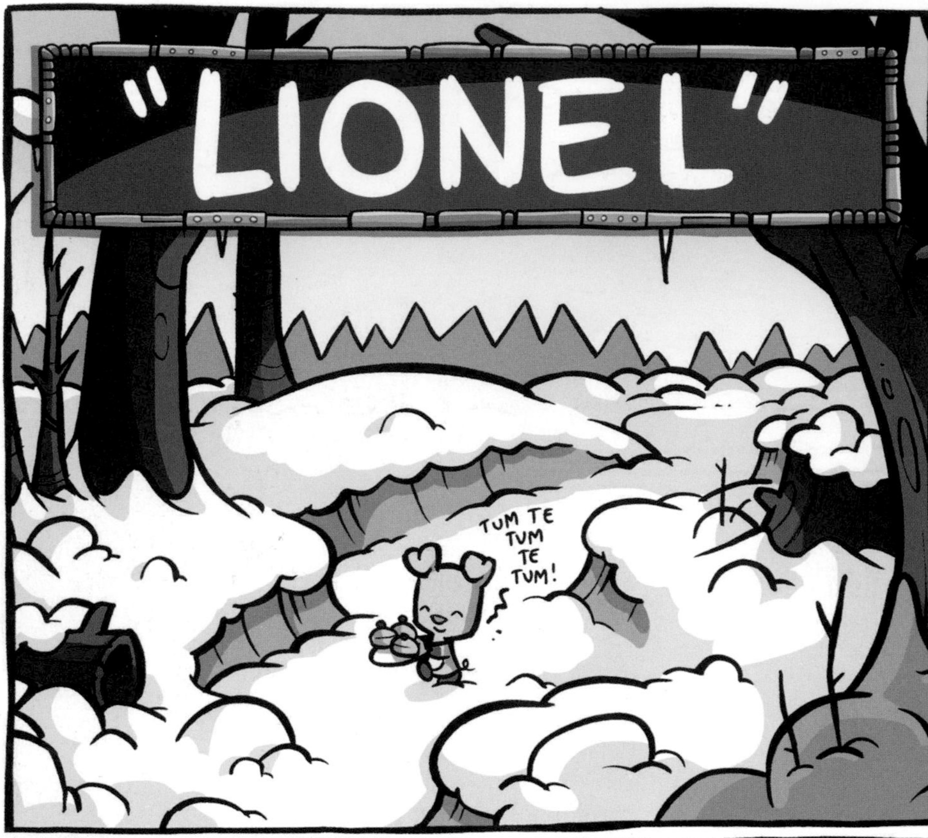

"LIONEL"

TUM TE TUM TE TUM!

EVERY DAY, I LEAVE MINCE PIES IN THE SAME SPOT, THEN WHEN I COME BACK HE'S EATEN THEM!

WHAT'S PIG DOING OUT HERE?
HE SAYS HE HAS AN IMAGINARY FRIEND!
HERE YOU GO, LIONEL. ENJOY!

UMM, PIG? YOU DO KNOW THOSE MINCE PIES ARE JUST GOING TO BE EATEN BY OTHER ANIMALS?
HA HA, NOT IF LIONEL GETS THERE FIRST!

HALF AN HOUR LATER...
THERE, YOU SEE? LIONEL ATE THEM ALL!
HEE HEE, SAME TIME TOMORROW, LIONEL!

NEXT DAY...
HEY, PIG! WE HEAR YOU HAVE AN IMAGINARY FRIEND!
LIONEL, YES.
HA HA. LIONEL.

IF I HAD AN IMAGINARY FRIEND, I'D CALL HIM... MONSTERTRUCKOTRON 4!
WHY 4?
THE PREVIOUS 3 FOUGHT EACH OTHER TO THE DEATH!

I THINK YOU'RE JUST EATING THOSE MINCE PIES YOURSELF, GREEDY PIG.
SO WE'RE GOING TO HANG AROUND, AND SEE WHAT HAPPENS.
AND WE HAVE A LITTLE 'SURPRISE' IN STORE FOR 'LIONEL'.
SCOOP!
WH... WHAT ARE YOU DOING?
IF LIONEL IS REAL, THESE ANGRY SNOWMEN WILL SCARE HIM OFF!
HAR HAR!
DON'T BE MEAN TO LIONEL!
NOW WE HIDE, AND WAIT UNTIL HE SHOWS UP!
OR DOESN'T EXIST.
OR DOESN'T EXIST, YES.
BRMMMMMM!
BANG! BANG!
VRRMMM!
HERE HE COMES! IT'S LIONEL!
WHAT, REALLY?

I, UM... I HAVE TO GO. WHATEVER LIONEL IS, I DON'T WANT TO BE HERE.
PANIC!
YOU SILLIES! I REFUSE TO BE SCARED OF SOMEONE CALLED LIONEL!

BANG!
PUTT PUTT!
BRMMM!

WAIT FOR ME!

BANG! BANG!
SCREEECH!

HELLO! MY NAME IS...
Lionel

MMM! MORE MINCE PIES...
...AUGH!
AUGH!
PARK RANGER

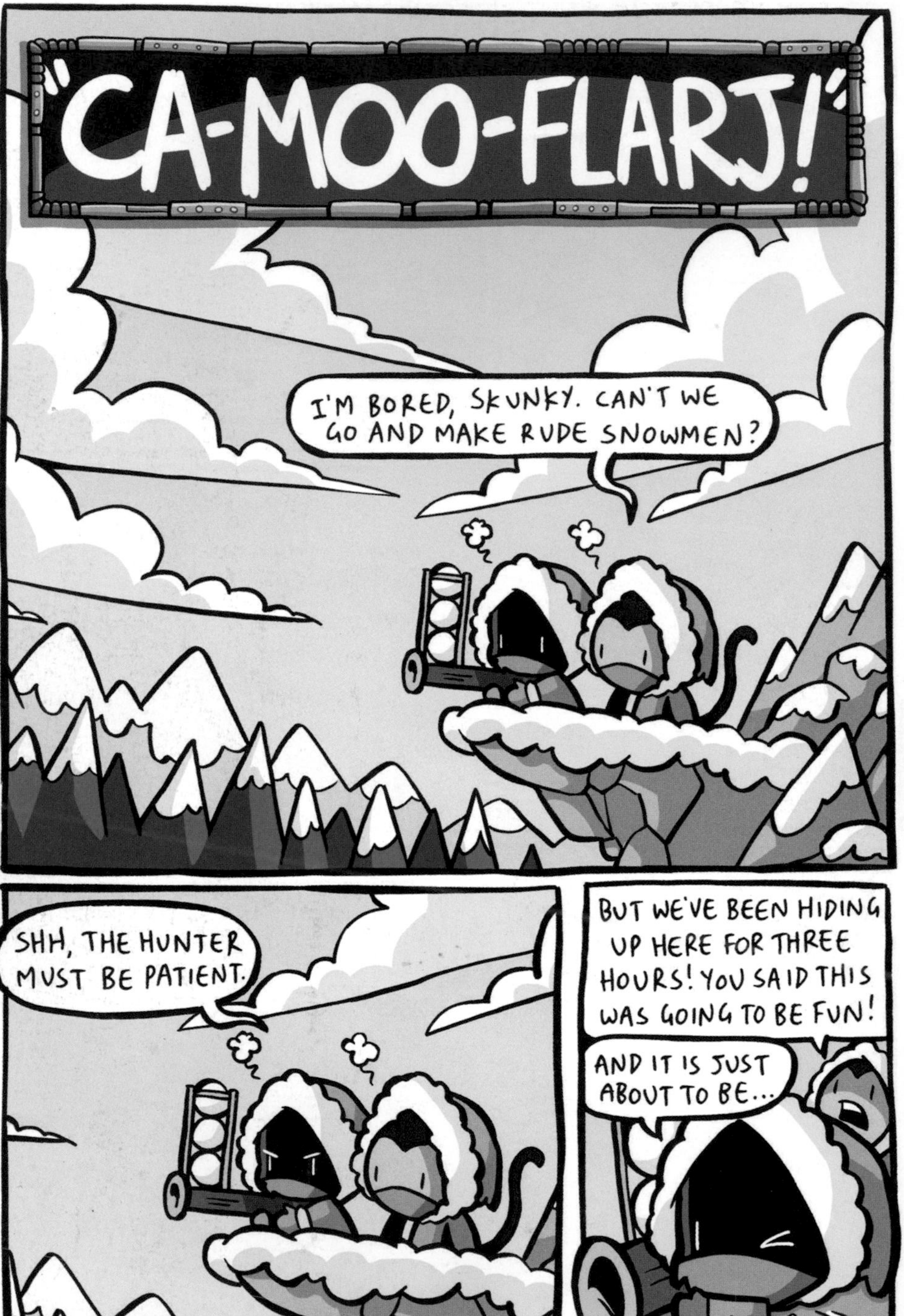

"CA-MOO-FLARJ!"

I'M BORED, SKUNKY. CAN'T WE GO AND MAKE RUDE SNOWMEN?

HERE THEY ARE! OUR PREY, INNOCENTLY GAMBOLLING IN THE SNOW, UNAWARE OF THEIR FATE.
LA LA LA!
DO IT NOW! NOW!
PTOOM! PTOOM! PTOOM!
AUGH! SNOWBALL ONSLAUGHT!
WHO...WHO'S THERE?
ANGELS?
QUICKLY, RELOAD! RELOAD!
WHILE WE ARE IN OUR WINTER SOLDIER CAMOUFLAGE, WE ARE PRACTICALLY INVISIBLE...
IS THAT SKUNKY?

AW BUM!
I CAN SEE YOU BOTH, AND THAT WAS VERY MEAN.
PIG NOW HAS SNOW UP HIS NOSE.
SNORT!

YOU CAN'T SEE US. WE BLEND INTO OUR SURROUNDINGS, ALL SECRETIVE AND STEALTHY!
PFFT. WE CAN HIDE BETTER THAN YOU!
HUFF!

QUICKLY, PIG! HIDE BEHIND A SHRUB OR SOMETHING!
HEE HEE!

HANG ON, WHERE DID THEY GO?
RRGH! NO ONE IS BETTER AT HIDING THAN ME! I WON'T HAVE IT!
GONE!

BEHOLD! MY PLAN B, THE CA-MOO-FLARJ! A HIGH-SPEED ROBOTIC BOVINE VEHICLE, FITTED WITH THE LATEST TECHNOLOGICAL SCREENING DEVICES TO RENDER IT INVISIBLE TO RADAR, SCANNER, AND THE NAKED EYE!

MOO.

OH, WHERE'S IT GONE?

VWOOP!

BOOP!

I'M JUST KIDDING, IT'S INVISIBLE. THAT'S THE POINT.

CLIMB ON, MONKEY! WE WILL DESCEND ON THEM AS HUSHED AS THE WIND!

PYEW! PYEW! PYEW!

WHIZZ!

WELL, WHERE IS EVERYONE?
DOOMF!
NO FAIR! WHO THREW THAT?
PLINK!
I'M...I'M NOT PLAYING ANY MORE.
OOF!
SHRIEK! WE'RE HOPELESSLY OUTGUNNED! RETREAT! RETREAT!
HA! SOME OF US ARE JUST SUITED TO THE SNOW NATURALLY!
MOOO!
JAM16

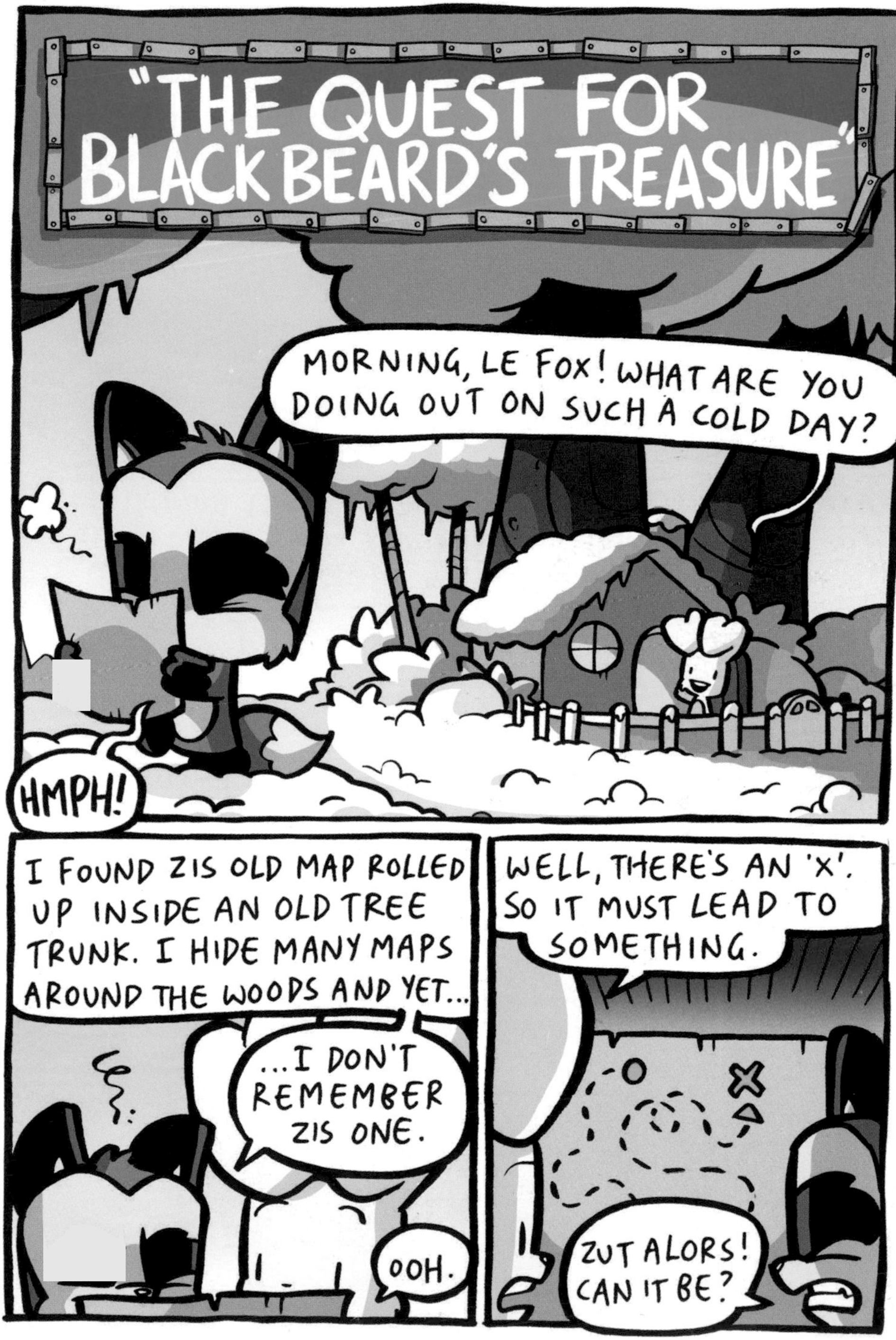

"THE QUEST FOR BLACKBEARD'S TREASURE"

MORNING, LE FOX! WHAT ARE YOU DOING OUT ON SUCH A COLD DAY?

HMPH!

WHEN I WAS A LITTLE FOX, MY FATHER TOLD ME ABOUT GREAT GREAT GRANDFATHER FOX, WHO SAILED TO OUR WOODS FROM ABROAD...

HE BROUGHT WITH HIM A CHEST FULL OF TREASURE! ON HIS LONG AND PERILOUS JOURNEY, HE HAD FOUGHT MANY PIRATES AND TAKEN THEIR GOLD AS REWARD.
SHINE!

FATHER SAID HE BURIED ZIS TREASURE SOMEWHERE IN THESE WOODS, BUT WE COULD NEVER WORK OUT WHERE!
PERHAPS ZIS IS THE MAP THAT TELLS US.

COME, LITTLE BUNNY! WE ARE ABOUT TO DISCOVER A **FORTUNE!**
WELL, I WAS GOING TO BAKE SOME SCONES.
BUT OKAY.

WHAT'S THAT? CAN I HAVE IT? IT LOOKS LIKE IT SAYS 'MONKEY' ON IT.
IT DOESN'T SAY MONKEY ON IT.
YOU SURE?

GIMME!
GAH! GET YOUR FILTHY SIMIAN PAWS OFF OUR TREASURE MAP...
OOPS!
SNATCH!

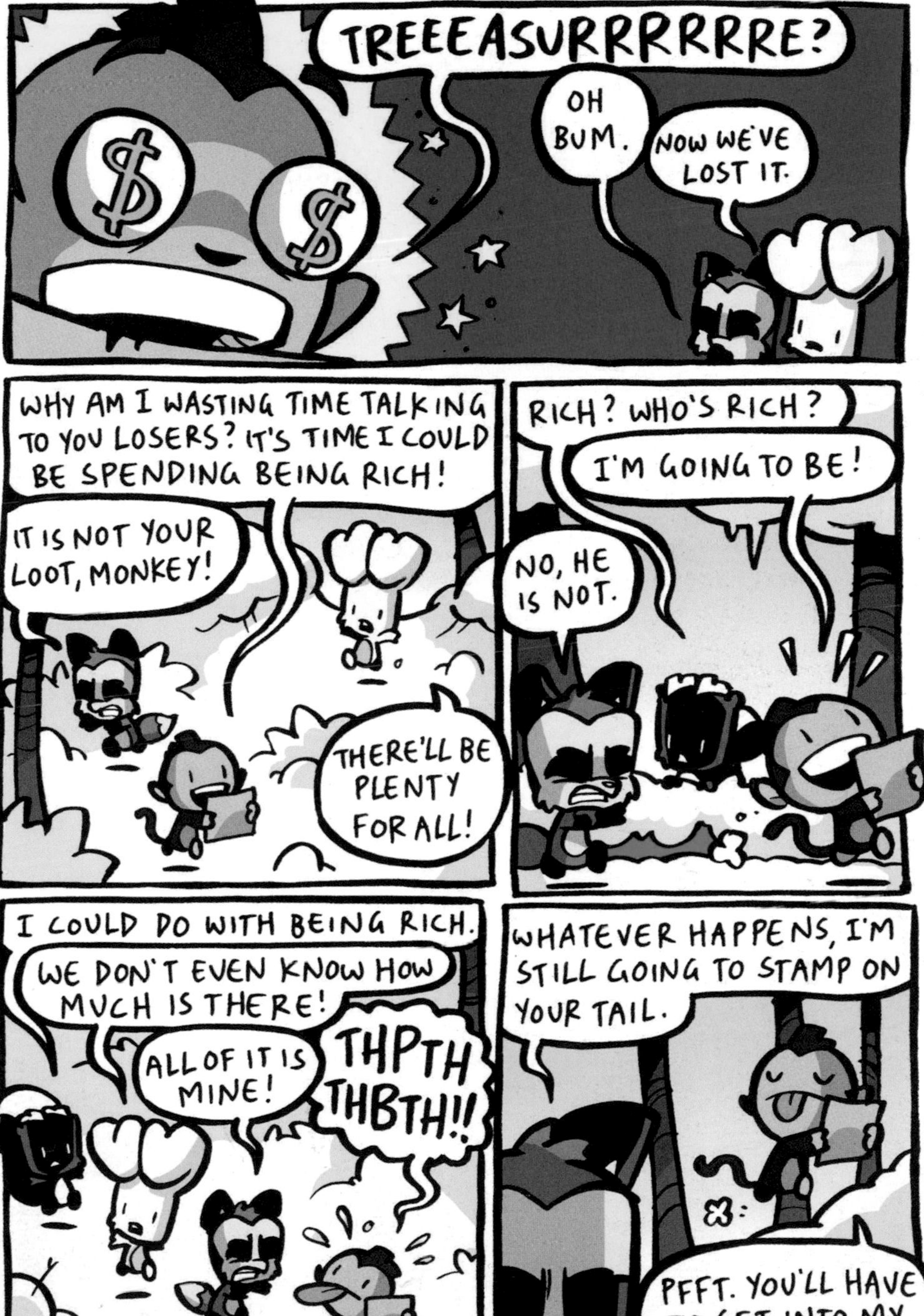

WHY AM I WASTING TIME TALKING TO YOU LOSERS? IT'S TIME I COULD BE SPENDING BEING RICH!

IT IS NOT YOUR LOOT, MONKEY!

THERE'LL BE PLENTY FOR ALL!

RICH? WHO'S RICH?

I'M GOING TO BE!

NO, HE IS NOT.

I COULD DO WITH BEING RICH.

WE DON'T EVEN KNOW HOW MUCH IS THERE!

ALL OF IT IS MINE!

THPTH THBTH!!

WHATEVER HAPPENS, I'M STILL GOING TO STAMP ON YOUR TAIL.

PFFT. YOU'LL HAVE TO GET INTO MY PALACE FIRST!

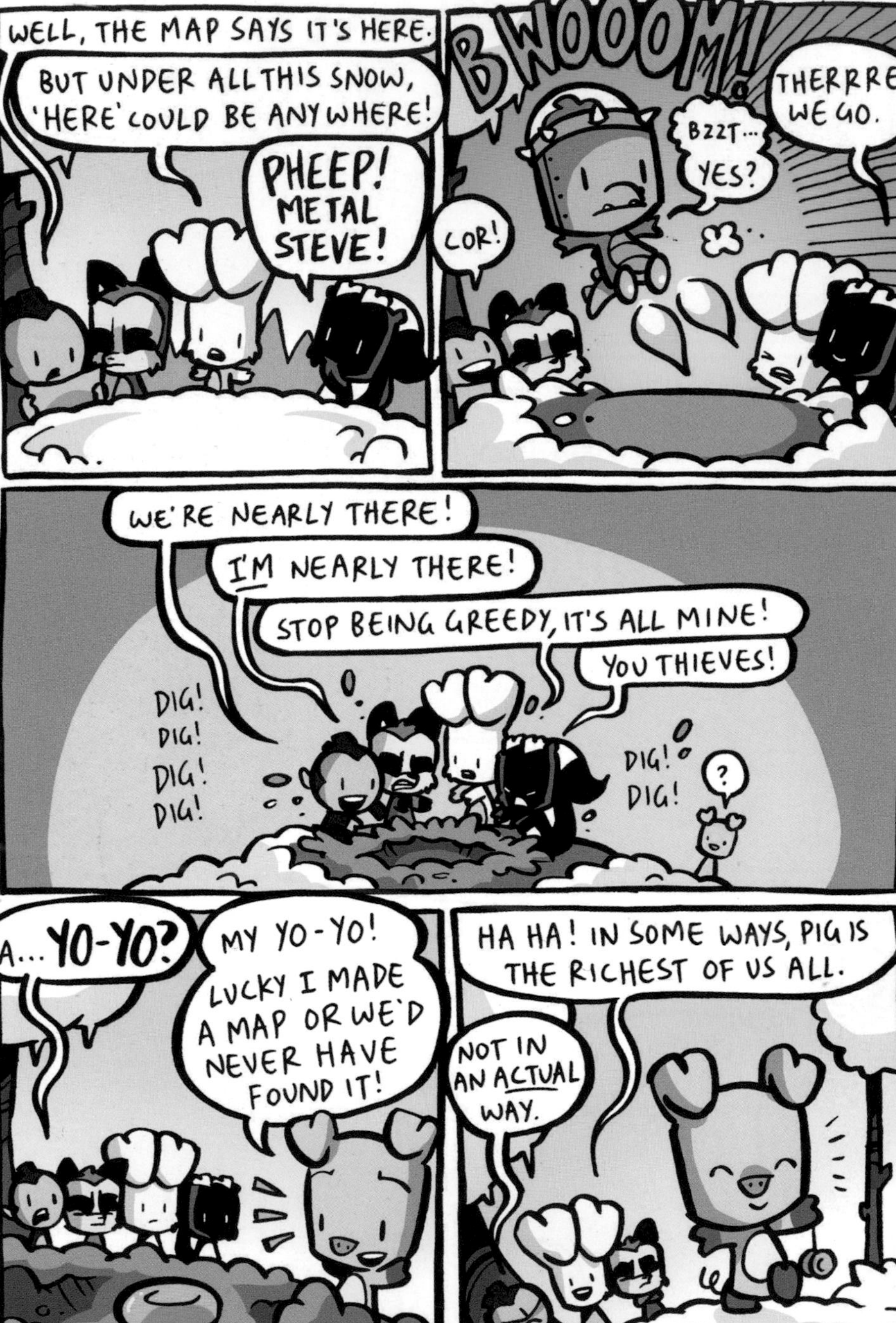

A... YO-YO?

MY YO-YO! LUCKY I MADE A MAP OR WE'D NEVER HAVE FOUND IT!

JAMIE

HA HA! IN SOME WAYS, PIG IS THE RICHEST OF US ALL.

NOT IN AN ACTUAL WAY.

"T3-DDY"
HOME SWEET HOME
HUSH, LITTLE SQUIRREL, AND FALL ASLEEP... TEDDY DOESN'T WANT TO HEAR A PEEP...
ZZZ...
TEDDY.
WHAT... ON EARTH?!
SHH! HE'S JUST DROPPING OFF!
AM I SEEING THINGS? AM I DREAMING? OR DID I JUST GO INSANE?
WEENIE'S BEEN HAVING TROUBLE SLEEPING, SO I'M HELPING HIM RELAX.
BUT... WHY?
WHY? I'LL TELL YOU WHY.

BECAUSE WHEN HE'S ASLEEP, I CAN HELP MYSELF TO ALL THE FOOD HE'S BEEN BAKING IN THE DAY!

MONKEY! I KNEW IT WAS TOO GOOD TO BE TRUE!
SCOFF...
MMM...
ECCLES CAKES!

THIS AIN'T NO TEDDY AT ALL!
THIS IS SKUNKY'S PATENTED T3-DDY MECHANOID! HAR HAR HARR!!
BOOP! BOOP!
YOU GET OUT OF THERE, OR THERE'LL BE TROUBLE.
OH, THERE'LL DEFINITELY BE TROUBLE...

THE T3-DDY IS FULLY WEAPONISED, AND **DESIGNED** FOR TROUBLE!
VUT!
PYEW!
PYEW!
PYEW!
STOMP!
STOMP!
STOMP!
ARRGHHH!

ALL WILL BOW IN FEAR, AS THIS LITTLE BEAR GOES PYEW PYEW PYEW, ALL THE WAY HOME!
HAR HAR HAR!
HUH?

HEY THERE, MISTER TEDDY. STOP BEING NAUGHTY.
ZZZ.
TUG!
GASP, IT'S WEENIE! AND HE'S SLEEP-WALKING!

COME ON NOW, BACK TO BED.
ZZZ.
BUT, I...
UM...
HA HA, YOU DON'T WANT TO BLOW YOUR COVER, MONKEY!

MAYBE YOU'LL BOTH GET A GOOD NIGHT'S SLEEP TONIGHT!
ZZZ.
RGH! I WAS DESTROYING!
DESTR-OYING!

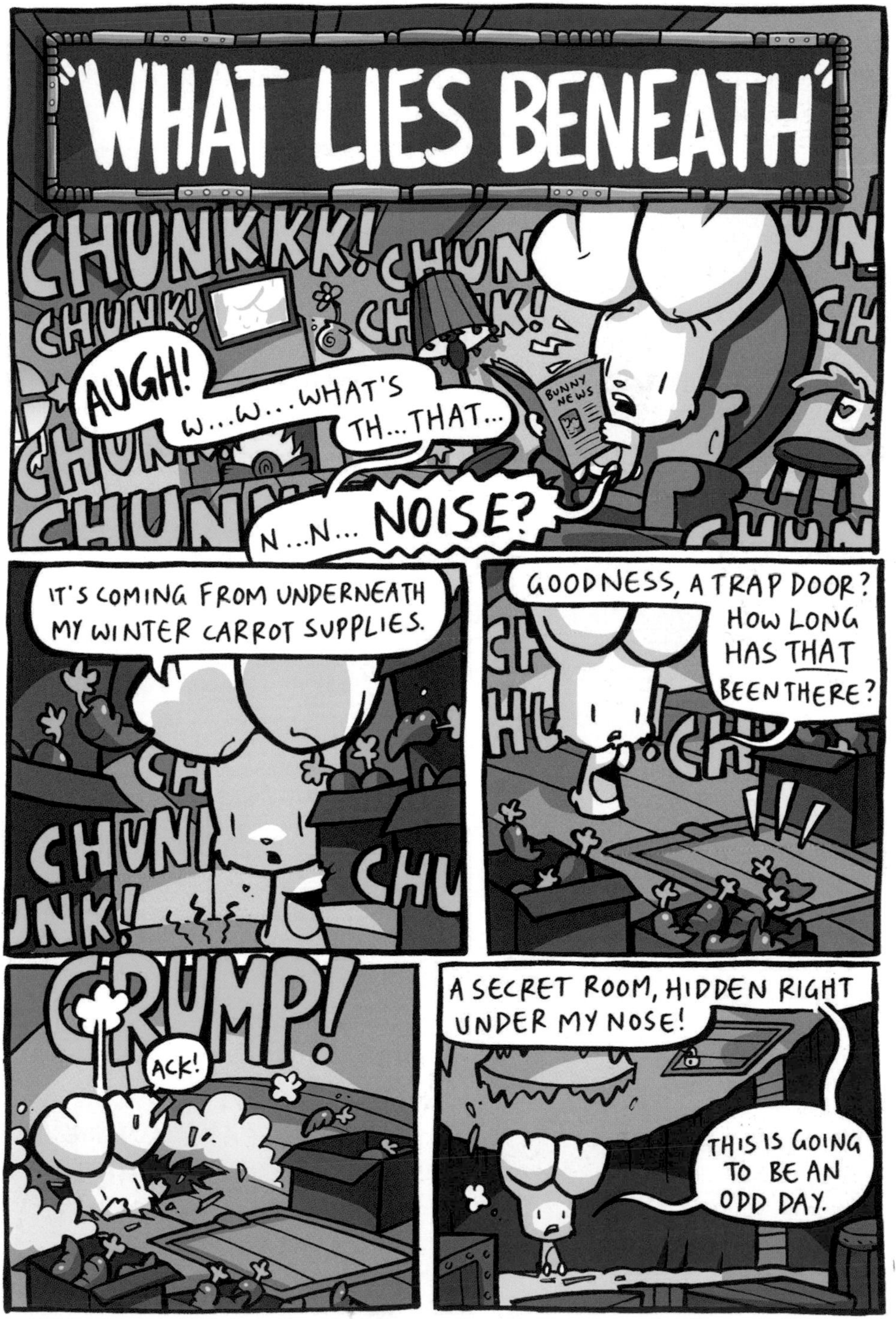

"WHAT LIES BENEATH"

CHUNKKK! CHUNK! CHUNK!
AUGH!
W...W...WHAT'S TH...THAT...
N...N... NOISE?
BUNNY NEWS

GASP... NOT JUST A SECRET ROOM... I'M IN SKUNKY'S LAIR!
SHUNK!
NKK!
DINNERTIME!

THERE YOU GO, FLOPSY. EAT UP, THERE'S PLENTY MORE WHERE THAT CAME FROM.
MIP!

SKUNKY! IS THAT THE WEIRD CREATURE YOU FOUND AT THE CENTRE OF THE EARTH?
EEK! INTRUDER!
OH, IT'S JUST BUNNY.

WHAT DO YOU MEAN 'JUST' BUNNY? ANYWAY, I DIDN'T INTRUDE, I FELL IN.
UH-OH. THE SNOZZIGATATRON MUST HAVE WEAKENED YOUR HOUSE FOUNDATIONS.
I SHOULDN'T HAVE SET IT TO MAXIMUM OVERDRIVE.

IT'S JUST FLOPSY, YOU SEE. TURNS OUT HE HAS A FEROCIOUS APPETITE FOR SAUSAGES, AND THE ONLY WAY I COULD KEEP HIM FED WAS TO INVENT A DEVICE TO PRODUCE SAUSAGES AT HIGH SPEED!
CHUNKK
GRAVEL
GRISTLE
GRIT
THUS, THE SNOZZIGATATRON!!

THAT'S WHAT'S BEEN MAKING ALL THE NOISE BENEATH MY FLOOR!
MY LAIR REACHES FAR AND WIDE UNDER THESE WOODS. IT'S NOT MY FAULT IF YOU LIVE ON TOP OF IT.

NOT YOUR FAULT? SKUNKY, EVERYTHING BAD THAT HAPPENS HERE IS YOUR FAULT.
CHUNK CHUNK!
NOW, HOW DO I TURN THIS THING OFF?
NOOOO!

IF YOU DEPRIVE FLOPSY OF HIS SAUSAGES, THERE'S NO TELLING WHAT HE'LL DO!
EAT SOMETHING ELSE, PROBABLY.
WELL, PROBABLY. BUT IS IT WORTH THE RISK?

THIS THING IS NOISY AND I WANT IT OFF!
NO! SAUSAGES!
THAT'S NOT AN ARGUMENT!
SAUSAGES!
MIP! MIP!
CHUNK!

#☆@☆ ✋ ⚡!!
CHUNK
CHUNK!
CHU

CHUNK!

CRUMBLE!
ARGH!

NOT THE SAUSAGES!!

HNUHFF!
GRAB!
YEEK!
CHUNK!
MAYBE YOU SHOULDN'T USE THIS PART OF YOUR LAIR, SKUNKY. THE GROUND IS FAR TOO UNSTABLE.
WHAT DO YOU KEEP IN HERE, ANYWAY?

I DIDN'T KNOW ANYTHING WAS DOWN THERE.
OH, AS IF, SKUNKY!

AN ENORMOUS CAVERN UNDER YOUR LAIR, ARE YOU SERIOUSLY TELLING ME YOU'RE NOT HIDING SOME TERRIBLE SECR...
CHUNK! CHUNK! CHUNK!

...WHAT'S THAT SMELL?
CHUNK! CHUNK!

AUGH! WHAT IS THAT? PULL ME UP!!
THEY'RE ONLY SAUSAGES!
THEY'RE NOT STRONG ENOUGH TO SUPPORT A...

SNAP!

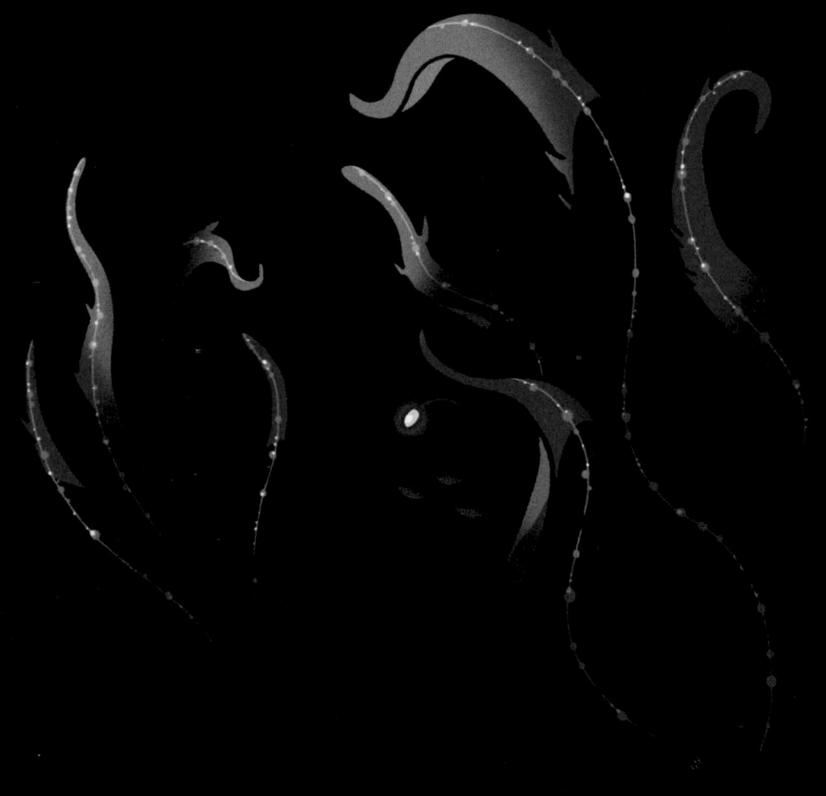
...BUNNY.

EEEEEEEE
UH?
DOOMF!
CHOMP!
CHOMP!
CHOMP!
MIP!
NOM!
MIP!
FLOPSY? YOU...
...INFLATED?

WOW. HE SURE DOES LIKE SAUSAGES.
BUT I DIDN'T KNOW HE DID THAT.

THPTHBTH!
HEE HEE! IT SOUNDS LIKE YOU FARTED!
RUN, SKUNKY!
FROM WHATEVER IS UNDERNEATH YOUR FLOOR!

OH.
OH YES.
SCARPER!

I AM NEVER, EVER, GOING BACK THERE AGAIN.
SHAKE!
BANG!
BANG!
BANG!

ONE DAY, FLOPSY, LET'S GO DOWN THERE AGAIN.
MIP!

SPRING

"CASA DEL PIG!"

PIG? IT'S CHUCKING IT DOWN OUT HERE, WHY AREN'T YOU AT HOME?

I AM!

THIS UMBRELLA IS MY HOME! WHATEVER THE WEATHER, IT KEEPS ME SAFE.
ALL THIS TIME... YOU'VE BEEN LIVING UNDER AN UMBRELLA?

THIS WON'T DO, PIG. YOU NEED A HOUSE! SOMEWHERE TO LIVE!

WHERE DO PIGS LIVE?

UM...

I DON'T KNOW! HOORAY! BUT I WILL **BUILD MYSELF A HOUSE,**

JUST LIKE THE REST OF YOU!

YAY!

FOOMPHH!

ONE RUSHED CONSTRUCTION LATER...
TAA DAA! A HOUSE IN THE TREES, JUST LIKE WEENIE!
I'VE ALWAYS WANTED A NEIGHBOUR!

URF...HUFF...OH, I FORGOT PIGS AREN'T VERY GOOD AT CLIMBING.
I CAN'T GET IN MY HOUSE!
SIGHH.

I COULD LIVE UNDERGROUND INSTEAD, JUST LIKE LE FOX!
I DON'T REMEMBER AGREEING TO ZIS.

HANG ON, YOU DIDN'T LEAVE ZE FRONT DOOR OPEN, DID YOU?
UMM...

YOU STUPID PIG! WHEN YOU LIVE UNDERGROUND, THE RAIN WASHES IN!
SPLLLOOOOSH!
WHEEE!
OH, YOU MEAN THIS IS A BAD THING.

A BIT LATER...
BUNNY, COME LOOK SEE! I'VE BUILT A HOUSE ON THE RIVER EXACTLY LIKE ACTION BEAVER!

'EXACTLY'? UH-OH.

YOU DO KNOW HOW ACTION BEAVER BUILDS HIS HOUSES, DON'T YOU? OUT OF TWIGS AND EXPLOSIVES.
TICK! TICK! TICK!
SSS..
TNT
TNT
UMM...

BO-OM!!!
EEE EE!!

HOW ABOUT METAL STEVE? WHERE DOES HE LIVE?
WHEEE OOMPH!

MAYBE NOT.
INSTALLING..

PIG, THIS IS CRAZY, WE MUST BE ABLE TO BUILD SOME SORT OF HOME THAT IS RIGHT FOR YOU.

NOT TO WORRY, BUNNY! THIS HAS GIVEN ME ALL I NEED...

CASA DEL PIG
...TO BUILD A HOUSE OUT OF THE MESS!
PIGS LOVE MESS!
HOORAY!
MAYBE GO INSIDE IT THEN?
OH...OH YES.
LOST

"MEET RANDOLPH!"

HAR HAR, THE **HELLIPHANT** IS YOUR BEST INVENTION YET, SKUNKY!

VVVMMMMMM!

THUMP! THUMP!

THUMP! THUMP! THUMP!

I CAN USE IT TO JUST SUCK EVERYONE ELSE UP!

SQUEEZE!
I'M RANDOLPH THE RACCOON, AND I THOUGHT IT WOULD BE NICE TO HAVE A HOLIDAY IN THE WOODS.
(CLEARLY NOT.)

COUSIN LE FOX?
OH.
BUM.

COUSIN? YOU CAN'T BE COUSINS. YOU'RE NOT EVEN FRENCH!
NEITHER'S HE!
ALL OF YOU, GO AWAY.

HOW'VE YOU BEEN, COUSIN? YOU SHOULD COME VISIT SOMETIME YOU KNOW, THERE'S SO MUCH FOOD!
YES, WELL, MAYBE.
A-HEM!

I'M STILL IN CHARGE OF A VERY POWERFUL HELLIPHANT, YOU KNOW! YOU SHOULD ALL BE RUNNING!
HUFF!

WH... WHAT ARE YOU DOING?
I AM ATTACHING ITS NOSE TO ITS TAIL.
YOU THINK YOU CAN DEFEAT ME?
AN ELEPHANT CAN'T SUCK ITS OWN TAIL.
WE SHALL SEE!
NO, MONKEY! THE HELLIPHANT'S PULL IS SO GREAT, IT WILL SUCK ITSELF INTO A QUANTUM SINGULARITY!
VMMMMMMMMMMMMMMMMMMMMMMMMMMMMMMMMMMMMMMMMMMM
MY INVENTION! WIPED FROM EXISTENCE!
HOW DID YOU KNOW TO DO THAT, RANDOLPH?
OBVIOUS, ISN'T IT? YOU LEARN A LOT OF COMMON SENSE ON THE STREETS.
WELL, IT HAS BEEN FUN AND ALL, BUT MAYBE I'LL HEAD HOME. ROUGHING IT OUT HERE CLEARLY ISN'T FOR ME.
HANG ON. 'STREETS'?
LE FOX! TEXT ME!
HMPH.

"THE STENCH!"

MINE'S BIGGER!
NO! MINE IS!
HEY, WHAT ARE YOU TWO DOING? CAN I JOIN IN?
I'VE DECIDED TO RENOUNCE EVIL!!

I'M TIRED OF THAT SHRIEKING MONKEY TELLING ME TO SHUT UP. SO THIS MORNING, I WOKE UP AND I THOUGHT 'HEY! I WANT TO BE GOOD FROM NOW ON!'

THAT'S WONDERFUL, MISTER SKUNKY! YOU CAN JUDGE OUR 'TALLEST SUNFLOWER' CONTEST!
WE'VE BEEN GROWING THEM FOR MONTHS! PROTECTING THEM FROM WINTER!
THEY'RE SO SPECIAL!

HMM, WELL, I'D SAY...
WILT!!
...OH NO!
WILT!!

THEY DIED-ED! WHY DID THEY DIE?
POO! I THINK IT WAS SKUNKY'S SMELL! HE STINKS!

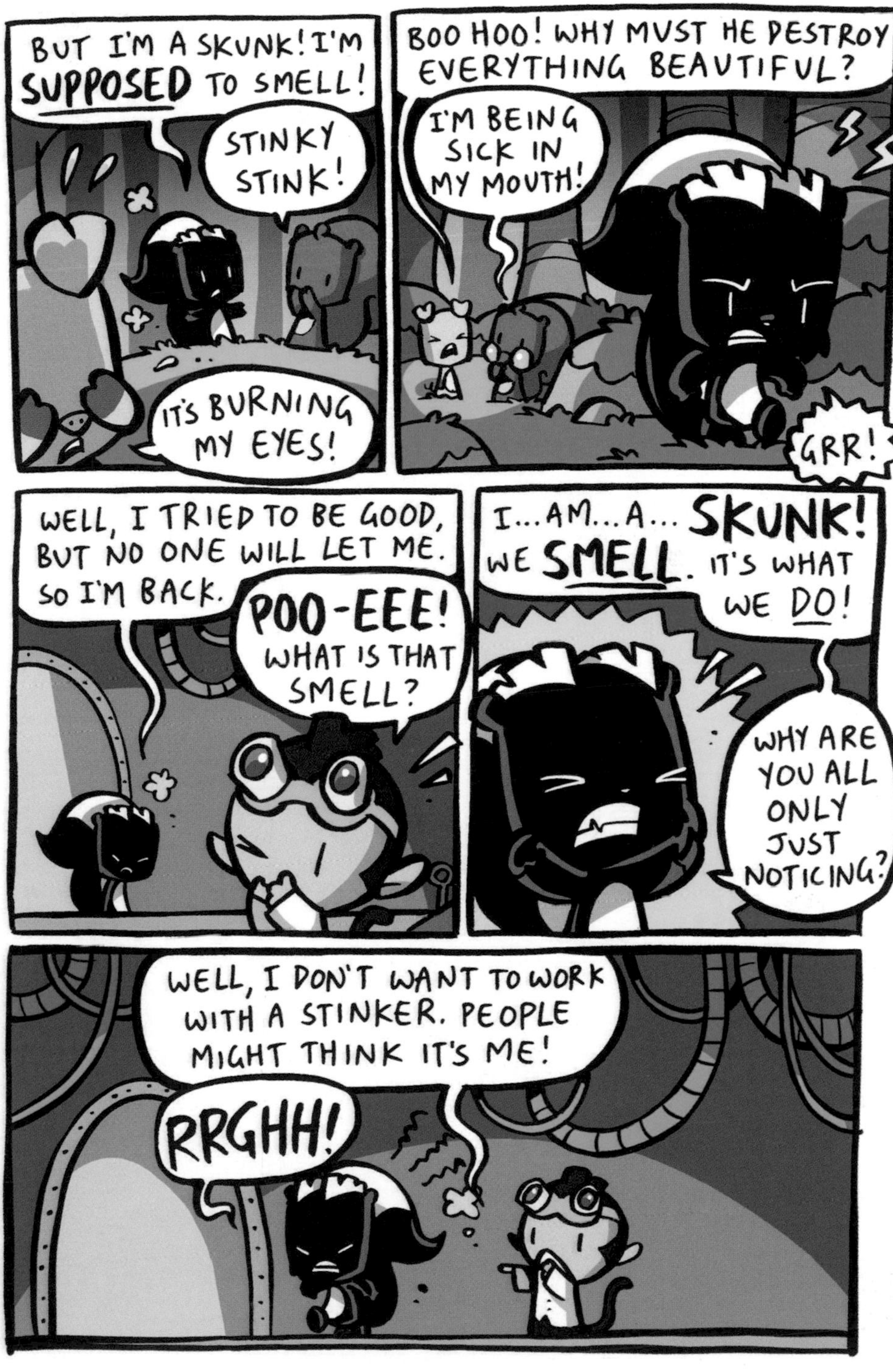

BUT I'M A SKUNK! I'M SUPPOSED TO SMELL!

STINKY STINK!

IT'S BURNING MY EYES!

BOO HOO! WHY MUST HE DESTROY EVERYTHING BEAUTIFUL?

I'M BEING SICK IN MY MOUTH!

GRR!

WELL, I TRIED TO BE GOOD, BUT NO ONE WILL LET ME. SO I'M BACK.

POO-EEE! WHAT IS THAT SMELL?

I... AM... A... SKUNK! WE SMELL. IT'S WHAT WE DO!

WHY ARE YOU ALL ONLY JUST NOTICING?

FINE! IF NO ONE WANTS ME, I MAY AS WELL GO FULL STINK!
I AM... THE STENCH!
WHIFFIEST SUPERVILLAIN IN THE WOODS! A STINKER BUT A THINKER, WITH A LOAD-A BAD ODOUR!
WILT!
WILT!
YOU WERE WRONG...
...TO DISMISS THE PONG!
MY SPECIALLY DESIGNED STINK SUIT BOOSTS MY SMELL BY 738%
AND THEN SPRAYS IT!
PSCHHH!!
HAR HAR HAR!
SCREAM!
EEK!
NOW IS THE STINKER OF MY DISCONTENT! HUARRGH!!

COUGH! COUGH! ARGH, I FORGOT, I'M STINKING INSIDE THE STINK SUIT.
POO, I DO SMELL!
IT'S CLOUDING MY VISION!

SPLOOSH!

OH, I SMELL MUCH BETTER! MAYBE ALL I NEEDED WAS A WASH!
GOOD. COME BACK TO BEING EVIL THEN.
JAMIE

OKAY. IT WAS A LOT MORE FUN!
AND SHUT UP.
SORRY.

"THE EDUCATING OF MISTER METAL STEVE"
SPRING HAS FINALLY SPRUNG IN THE WOODS, AND METAL STEVE IS MAKING THE MOST OF THE FINE WEATHER BY FISHING...
BZZT! BZZT! DESTROY!
BZZT! BZZT!
...WITH HIS EYE LASERS!!
BZZT! BZZT!
HUH?
IF FOUND, PLEASE RETURN TO:

Hello.
My name is
Elouise. I am 8.
If you find this
letter, please
write back and
let's be friends!
x x x

WHAT'S WRONG, METAL STEVE?
BZZT! WANT TO REPLY TO LETTER. BUT DON'T KNOW HOW TO WRITE!

THEN I WILL TEACH YOU!
BZZT! HOORAY!
BZZT!
YOW!
SORRY, HABIT.

A B C D E F G

BZZZT!!
!!

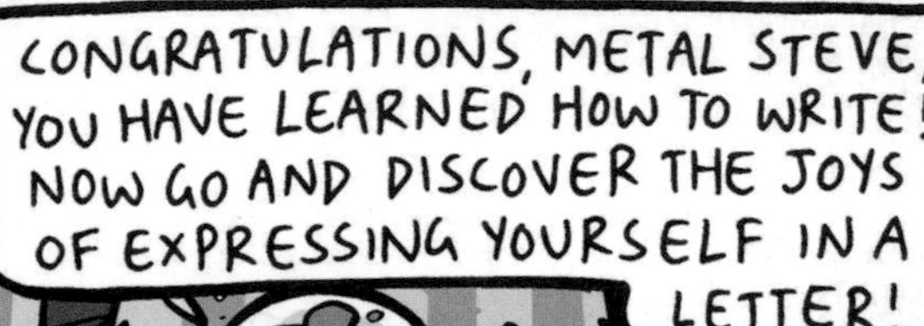
CONGRATULATIONS, METAL STEVE, YOU HAVE LEARNED HOW TO WRITE! NOW GO AND DISCOVER THE JOYS OF EXPRESSING YOURSELF IN A LETTER!

SCRIBBLE!
SCRIBBLE!
SCRIBBLE!

A FEW DAYS LATER...
MORNING, YOUNG LADY. IS THIS YOURS?
17
A REPLY!

FLUFFY ANIMALS!

BZZT! BZZT! DESTROY! BZZT!

"FISHY PLOPS!"

WHAT... IS IT?

IS IT A FISH?

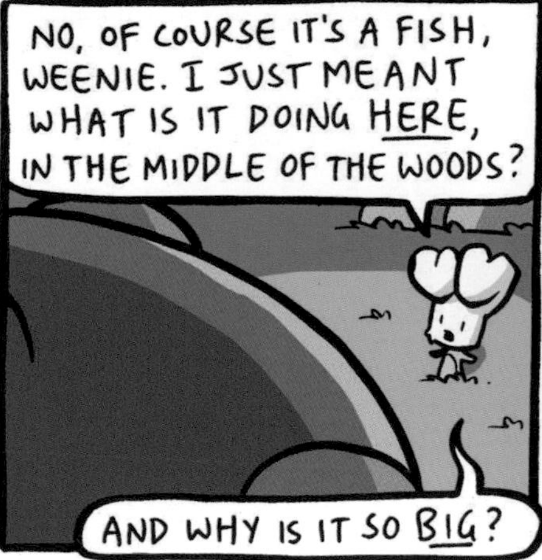

NO, OF COURSE IT'S A FISH, WEENIE. I JUST MEANT WHAT IS IT DOING HERE, IN THE MIDDLE OF THE WOODS?
AND WHY IS IT SO BIG?

FRRPP!
HEE HEE, IT'S ALL SQUISHY!
NICE TO CUDDLE!
FISH CUDDLES!
SORRY, BUT WE HAVE TO PUT IT BACK.

BACK WHERE?
IN THE RIVER. IT'S A FISH, IT BELONGS IN WATER.

MORNING!
SKUNKY! MONKEY! I SHOULD HAVE KNOWN THIS HAS SOMETHING TO DO WITH YOU.
WELL, WHATEVER IT IS, WE'RE DRAGGING IT BACK TO THE RIVER.

OH, THAT'S JUST FISHYPLOPS. A GIANT METAL FISH I CREATED, WRAPPED IN SYNTHETIC SKIN.
WHAT... WHAT DOES IT DO?

NOTHING.
NOTHING?
LITERALLY, NOTHING.

DRAG!!
HEEEAVE!!
PUFF PUFF!
HEAVE!
DRAG!
DRAG!

I'M SO TIRED, BUNNY.
SOB!
I CAN'T GO ON!
A FEW INCHES MORE! WE CAN ROLL IT DOWN THE RIDGE!
JUST A BIT MORE!

HRRGHH!
OOPS.
TEE HEE!
TUMBLE!
ARGH!

SPLOSH!
HE'S HOME!
YAYYYY!!
HOPEFULLY IT'LL DRIFT OUT TO SEA. WHAT AN ODD THING.

I STILL DON'T GET IT. WHY WOULD SKUNKY INVENT SOMETHING USELESS? A BIG DEAD FISH WHICH DOES... NOTHING?

WAS IT A PRESENT?
DID WE JUST THROW A PRESENT AWAY?

NO, YOU SUCKERS...

... IT WAS A DECOY, TO DISTRACT YOU LONG ENOUGH FOR ME TO WRITE BUM ON ALL YOUR STUFF!
HAR HAR HAR!
BUM
BUM
BUM
BUM
WELL, AT LEAST NOW WE KNOW.

"BAD CROWD!"

I AM **THE MONKEY!** THE MONKEY, THE MONKEY, THE MONKEY. THE **MONKEY!!**

EMPEROR OF THE WOODS! MEANIE OF THE FORESTS! **TYRANT OF NATURE!**

YOU! SILLY LITTLE FLYING WORM! BOW TO YOUR EMPEROR!

BOW TO EMPEROR MONKEY!

RRGH! BUMS TO YOU, THEN! **RRRGHH!**

HOI.

KICK! KICK!

WHAT? YOU CAN'T TELL ME WHAT TO DO!
GRUNT.
YES I CAN.

DON'T YOU KNOW WHO I AM?
NO.
WHAT? WHY NOT? I JUST DID A SONG ABOUT IT AND EVERYTHING.
GRUNT.
YOU SEEM LIKE AN IDIOT.

RIGHT! I'VE HAD ENOUGH OF YOU! PREPARE FOR SOME...
MONKEY MANIA!!

STOP... SHOUTING.
YES, SIR.
SORRY, SIR.

I'M BRICK, WE'RE WARTHOGS, AND WE ARE THE MEANEST, ROUGHEST, TOUGHEST ANIMALS IN THE WOODS.
GURR.
SNORT!

AND YOU ARE?
M...M... MONKEY. I'M GOING TO TAKE OVER THE WOODS AND ENSLAVE EVERYONE.

HAW HAW HAW! I DON'T FINK SO!
I AM! I JUST NEED TO GET THAT PESKY BUNNY OUT OF THE WAY FIRST.
GRUNT.
WHO?
STOMP! STOMP!

A BUNNY RABBIT? YOU'RE BEING CONSTANTLY DEFEATED... BY A BUNNY RABBIT?
WELL, WHEN YOU PUT IT LIKE THAT...

GO OVER THERE, AND PUSH HIM IN THE MUD!
PAINT HIM PURPLE!
TIE HIS EARS TO HIS FEET!
ARGH! TOO MUCH PEER PRESSURE!

WELL, DO SOMETHING, OR ARE YOU SCARED?
I'M NOT SCARED!
'E'S SCARED!
I'M NOT!
SCARED!

I'M NOT SCARED OF YOU!! HRRGH!!

BLAM!!

MONKEY, ARE YOU OKAY? WHAT'S WRONG WITH YOU?
THEY... THEY BULLIED ME!
I THINK I BROKE MY NOSE.

WHO? WHO BULLIED YOU?
THE UGLY PIGS OVER THERE!
WHAT UGLY PIGS?
GONE!

COME INSIDE, MONKEY. I THINK YOU BANGED YOUR HEAD.
I'M NOT SCARED OF YOU!
I KNOW.

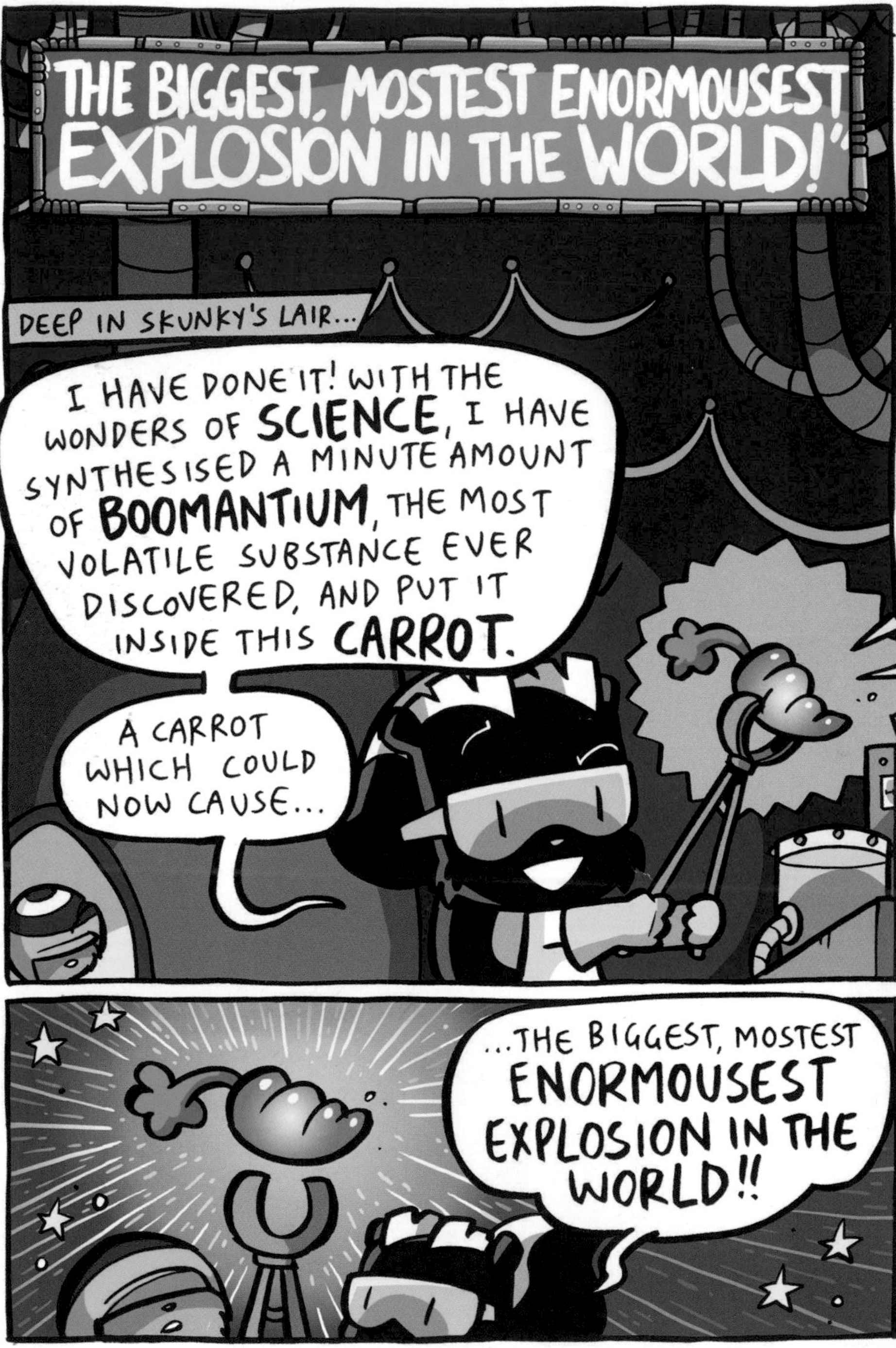

"THE BIGGEST, MOSTEST ENORMOUSEST EXPLOSION IN THE WORLD!"

DEEP IN SKUNKY'S LAIR...

I HAVE DONE IT! WITH THE WONDERS OF **SCIENCE**, I HAVE SYNTHESISED A MINUTE AMOUNT OF **BOOMANTIUM**, THE MOST VOLATILE SUBSTANCE EVER DISCOVERED, AND PUT IT INSIDE THIS **CARROT**.

A CARROT WHICH COULD NOW CAUSE...

WOOF!
NO, ACTION BEAVER. KEEP AWAY! THIS IS MY SECRET WEAPON, SHOULD MONKEY EVER GET OUT OF CONTROL, THE THREAT OF THIS CARROT WILL KEEP HIM IN LINE.

SUCH A POWERFUL VEGETABLE MUST BE KEPT LOCKED AWAY, SAFE AND UNDISTURBED.
COSY!

AHH, WHO'M I KIDDING? I WANT TO SHOW OFF HOW BRILLIANT I AM.

ABOVE GROUND...
LOOK, EVERYONE! THIS CARROT COULD CAUSE THE BIGGEST, MOSTEST ENORMOUSEST EXPLOSION IN THE WORLD!
AND I MADE IT WITH SCIENCE!

THIRTY SECONDS LATER...
PUT IT BACK!
IT'S DANGEROUS!
IT'S MINE!
CAN I PUT IT UP MY NOSE?
OWEE! OWEE!
SIGHHH.
YOU'D THINK I'D HAVE LEARNED BY NOW.

GIVE IT HERE! DON'T YOU REALISE THIS CARROT COULD CAUSE THE BIGGEST, MOSTEST...
OOPS!

TICK!
TICK!
TICK!
TICK!

EVERYBODY RUN AWAY! THE EXPLOSION WILLBE SO BIG, IT'LL KNOCK WHAT'S LEFT OF THE EARTH INTO SPACE!

TICK!
TICK!

CHOMP!
ACTION BEAVER, DON'T EAT IT!

BOOOOM!!
MERK.

I DON'T BELIEVE IT! ACTION BEAVER JUST SAVED THE WORLD... BUT HOW?
LET'S FIND OUT!
MORE SCIENCE!
SIGHH..

"BILLION DOLLAR BEAVER!"
ALL I CAN SMELL IS BURNING FUR!
WE'RE NOT DOING THIS FOR FUN, MONKEY. WE'RE TESTING ACTION BEAVER'S RESISTANCE TO THE BIGGEST LASER IN MY LABORATORY!
PING PING!
NOPE, NOT EVEN A SCRATCH. I DON'T UNDERSTAND IT, HE'S INDESTRUCTIBLE.
CLANG!!
FRRP!
MONKEY!

IT'S THE MOST POWERFUL CHEMICAL EVER SYNTHESISED, AND SOMEHOW IT MUST HAVE GOT INSIDE HIM.

I HAVE ACCIDENTALLY CREATED A **SUPER BEAVER!**

TARP!
ARR!
BOSH!
STICK HIM ON THE FRONT OF AN ALL-TERRAIN PIRATE SHIP AND SMASH THROUGH THE WOODS! OF COURSE!
ARR! WHY'S HE SPARKLING LIKE THAT, CAP'N?
HAR HARR! THE PUNY TREES STAND NO CHANCE AGAINST THE MIGHT OF A CHEMICALLY ALTERED BEAVER'S BONCE!
OH NO! I FEARED THIS MIGHT HAPPEN! CHEMICAL X IS HIGHLY VOLATILE, IF THE PARTICLES GET TOO OVER-EXCITED, THEY'RE LIABLE TO...
WHIZZZZZZ!
CRASH!
FWOOM!
FFT!
...COMBUST!
WE'RE GOING TOO FAST! WE CAN'T STOP!
THE FLAMES ARE SINGEING MY NOSE! ARR!
BBBB.
I MEAN, ARGH!

OUR ONLY CHANCE IS TO CRASH INTO THE RIVER BEFORE BUNNY'S HOUSE!

SCREAM!!
SCREAM!
SCREAM!
BUM.
BOSH!
JAMIE

STRANGE HOW YOUR SCIENTIFIC EXPERIMENTS OFTEN END IN ACTION BEAVER BEING ON FIRE.
SORRY, BUNNY.
SORRY, BUNNY.

THE KAKAPO POO KABOOM!
?
KA BOOM!
WHAT WAS THAAAAT? IT WOKE ME UP FROM MY SECOND MORNING NAP!
I'M NOT SURE...
...BUT I'LL BET IT'S SOMETHING TO DO WITH SKUNKY.

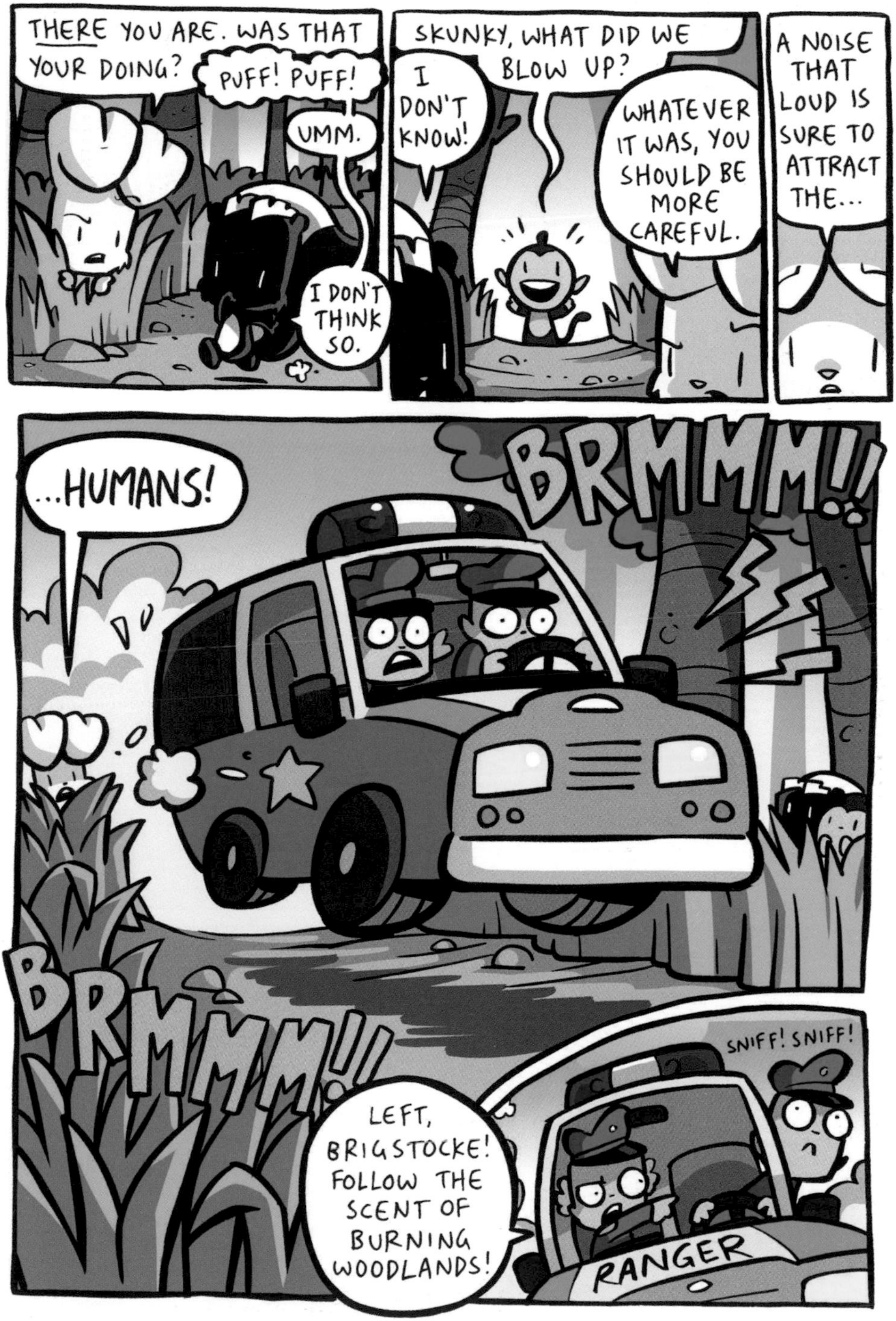

...HUMANS!

BRMMMM!!!

BRMMMM!!!

SNIFF! SNIFF!

LEFT, BRIGSTOCKE! FOLLOW THE SCENT OF BURNING WOODLANDS!

RANGER

DO YOU THINK THIS WAS WHERE THE EXPLOSION HAPPENED, SIR?

AT A GUESS.

GASP! LOOK AT IT, WHAT COULD HAVE POSSIBLY CAUSED SUCH DESTRUCTION?

DARNED KAKAPO.

I SEE YOU, UP THERE, CAUSING ALL THIS TROUBLE.

THE BIRDS, SIR?

NO, BRIGSTOCKE, THEIR POO! DARNED BIRDS EAT FERMENTED BERRIES, DO POOS FILLED WITH ETHANOL AND METHANE, THEN ONE SPARK AND...
KA-BOOM!
I'VE SEEN IT HAPPEN BEFORE.

EXPLOSIVE POO? THIS IS THE GREATEST DAY OF MY LIFE!
KING KAKAPO? HELLO?

IF THIS IS ABOUT THE POO, WE'RE NOT GOING TO STOP POOING.
I KNOW, BUT MAYBE STOP IT PILING UP?

IT HAS A TENDENCY TO BLOW UP. AND THAT ATTRACTS HUMANS.
FRRP!
WHO CARES? THIS IS GREAT!

IT WON'T BE SO GREAT WHEN THE HUMANS DISCOVER US. AND BY 'US', I MEAN YOU. AND BY 'YOU', I MEAN YOUR INVENTIONS.
NOT MY INVENTIONS! WHAT CAN WE DOOOO?

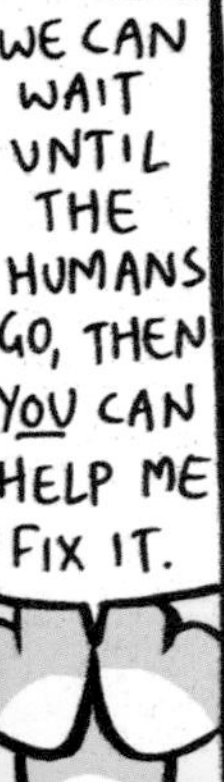
WE CAN WAIT UNTIL THE HUMANS GO, THEN YOU CAN HELP ME FIX IT.

A FEW WEEKS LATER...
WHAT.
THE.
A FULLY PLUMBED TOILET FOR BIRDS IS HARDLY MY GREATEST SCIENTIFIC ACHIEVEMENT.
I THINK IT'S PRETTY COOL, SKUNKY.

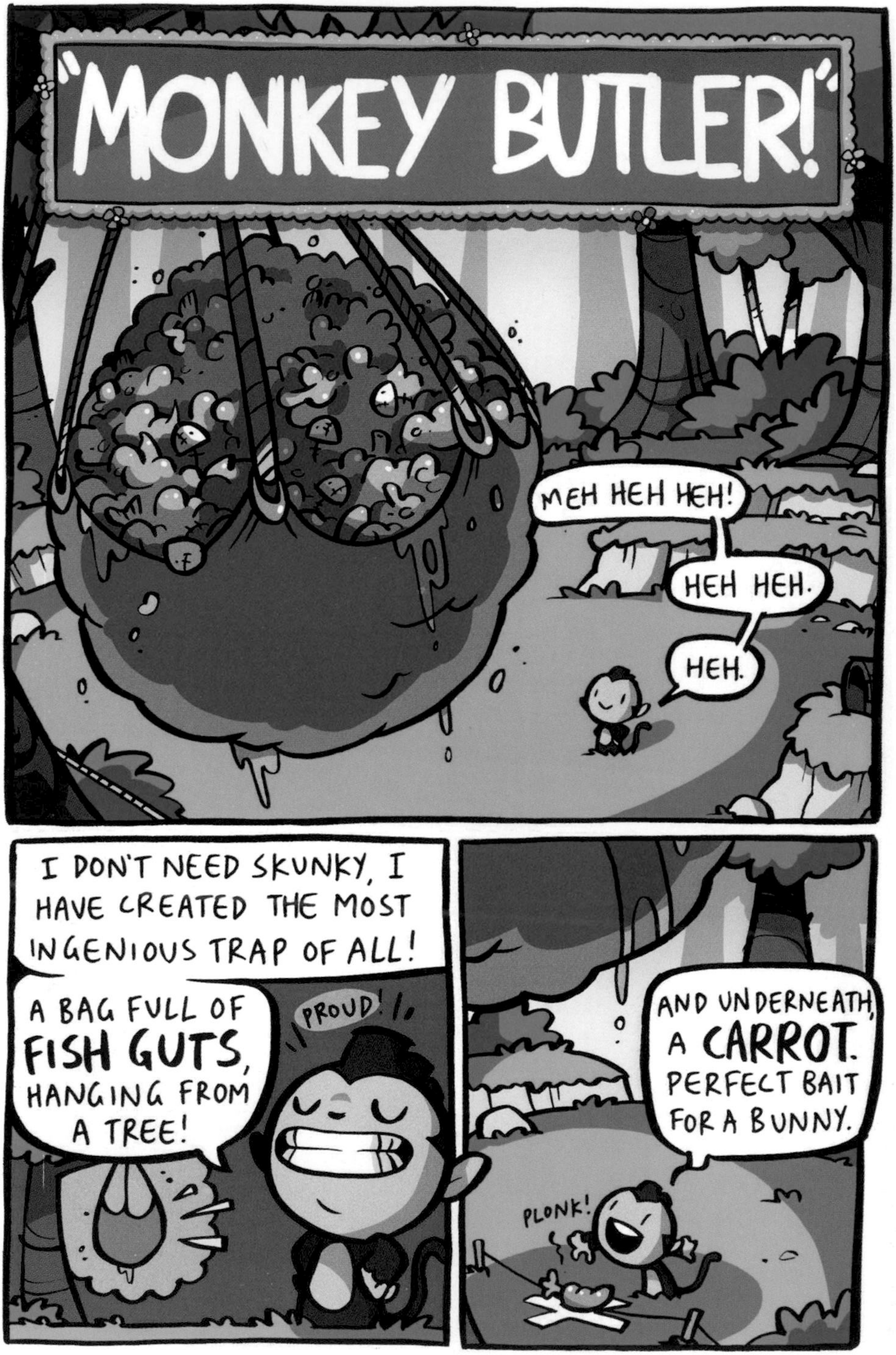

"MONKEY BUTLER!"

MEH HEH HEH!
HEH HEH.
HEH.

MISTER MONKEY! WHAT ARE YOU DOING?
I, UM...
WAIT...
WHAT ARE YOU DOING?

I AM LORD PIG PIGGINGTON OF PIGGYSHIRE!
AND I AM LADY WEENIE WHUFFINGTON WEENIE-ON-THE-WUFF.
WE ARE PLAYING POSH!

LOOK, I CAN'T HAVE YOU TWO SPOILING MY INGENIOUS TRAP. I NEED YOU TO NOT TELL ANYONE ABOUT THIS, OKAY?
HMM, WHAT IS IT WORTH, PEASANT?

SIGHHHH...
...ANYTHING. I'LL DO ANYTHING.
TEE HEE! THEN WE HAVE A SPLENDID IDEA!

TING-A-LING-A-LING-A-LING!
I SAY?
I SAY?

GRRR! WHAT IS IT, YOUR LORDSHIP?
I ASKED YOU TO BRING ME TOAST OVER HALF AN HOUR AGO, **MONKEY BUTLER!**

YEAH, WELL, YOU ONLY GAVE ME A TABLE LAMP TO HEAT THE BREAD WITH... OW!
BOP!
DON'T TALK BACK, MONKEY BUTLER! KNOW YOUR PLACE!

GASP! FISH GUTS!
PLOOMP!

HAR HAR! SO LONG, POSHOS! I **QUIT!** THIS MONKEY IS **NO ONE'S** BUTLER!

BUNNY? YOU'RE NOT COVERED IN FISH GUTS!
I SHOULD HOPE NOT.
B... BUT... THE CARROT!

I THOUGHT THAT MIGHT BE A TRAP. LUCKILY, I DON'T EVEN LIKE CARROTS.
BUT IF YOU DIDN'T SPRING THE TRAP, THEN WHO...?
I PREFER PIE.

I DON'T BELIEVE IT, THE ONE DAY I DECIDE TO EAT HEALTHILY, AND I GET THIS!
GASP!
IS THIS YOUR DOING, MONKEY? THAT'S IT, I'M NEVER HELPING YOU EVER AGAIN!

NO! ARGH! I'M SORRY, SKUNKY! MY INVENTIONS ARE STUPID! DON'T LEAVE ME! DON'T LEEEEEEEEEAVE ME!
WELL, THERE IS ONE THING YOU COULD DO...

HAT BACK ON.
JAMIE

COME, MONKEY BUTLER! COME AND HELP ME SCRUB FISH GUTS OUT OF MY FUR!
EUGHH.

"THE BIG EYE AM!"
GIANT EYEBALL!
WHAT?
WHERE DID THAT THING COME FROM?
WE DON'T KNOW!
WE JUST FOUND IT!
FWINGG!!
SO WE PUT A PIRATE HAT ON IT, AND CALLED IT CAPTAIN PIRATE!
CAP'N PIRATE EYE!
IT'S A P-EYE-RATE!
EYE EYE, CAP'N!
I DON'T KNOW WHAT WE'RE SAYING ANY MORE.
WHY DID YOU ROLL IT DOWN THE HILL? IT'S SMASHING THROUGH THE WOODS!

THAT'S NOT OUR FAULT! IT JUST RAN AWAY!
ARGH! IT FOUND ME!
WHY WON'T IT LEAVE ME ALONE?
MONKEY, YOU KNOW THIS EYE?
ONLY BECAUSE IT ZAPPED ME WITH ITS LASER VISION!
ZZAP!
ARGH!
OH YEAH, IT HAS LASER VISION.
ARGH!
AH. YOU FOUND IT.
ZZAP!
LE FOX! THIS IS YOURS?
NO. I FOUND THAT EYE SITTING IN A TREE FOR SOME REASON. WELL, I THOUGHT, WHEN YOU FIND A GIANT LASER-SHOOTING EYEBALL, WHAT DO YOU DO WITH IT?
HMM
WHY, YOU LEAVE IT OUTSIDE MONKEY'S FRONT DOOR, OF COURSE!
ZZAP!
HEH HEH.
ARGH!

WHAT A MEAN THING TO DO!
YOU WOULD HAVE DONE ZE SAME!
HEH HEH. I WOULD, YEAH.
SO, WAIT. YOU ALL FOUND THE EYE AT SOME POINT, BUT WHO ROLLED IT?
UMM..
BUMP!
CRR EEE EAK!
OOP.
WAIT WAIT WAIT. SO, LE FOX FOUND IT FIRST, THEN MONKEY, THEN PIG AND WEENIE, BEFORE METAL STEVE BUMPED IT DOWN THE HILL.
BUT WHERE DID IT COME FROM IN THE FIRST PLACE?

OH, BUNNY.
CRASHH!
OH, BUNNY, YOU HAD TO ASK.
YARGHH!! GIVE IT BACK!
A GIANT EYE COMES FROM WHATEVER'S MISSING A GIANT EYEBALL!!
SCREAMMM!
ARGH!
ZZZAP!

"ON THE ROAD!"
LE FOX, WHY ARE WE SITTING UNDERGROUND, IN THE DARK?
SHH! WE ARE DOING IMPORTANT THINGS.
SECRET... IMPORTANT THINGS.
HEY, GUYS, WHY ARE YOU IN THE DARK?
RANDOLPH!
ZUT! HE FOUND US.
YOU'RE NOT AVOIDING ME, ARE YOU, COUSIN?
YES, I WAS. YOU ARE VERY ANNOYING.

BY THE WAY, IS THIS DUDE YOUR FRIEND? I FOUND HIM STUCK IN A SINK-HOLE, RUNNING ROUND IN CIRCLES.
KEEP RUNNING! THEY'RE COMING!

HAMSTER 3000! HE WAS ZOOMING THROUGH THE WOODS LAST YEAR, SAYING THE SAME THING.
ACTUALLY, THAT IS WHY I'M HERE. YOU SHOULD HAVE LISTENED TO HIM.

HE MEANS THE HUMANS. THEY ARE COMING.
PLANS FOR A-92
AND THEY'RE DOING IT BY ROAD!

PFFT! WE DON'T HAVE ANY ROADS HERE IN THE WOODS.
EXACTLY, THEY'RE GOING TO BUILD ONE.
RIGHT THROUGH YOUR HOMES.

I FOUND THESE PLANS IN AN ARCHITECT'S BIN. THEY'RE COMING FROM THE CITY, HERE, AND BUILDING A MOTORWAY TO REACH THE NEXT CITY, HERE. ONLY YOUR WOODS ARE IN THE WAY, SO THEY'LL HAVE TO BULLDOZE YOU.
UNDERSTAND?

LET ME GET THIS STRAIGHT.
WHAT'S A 'CITY'?
SIGHH.

CITIES ARE WHERE HUMANS LIVE, BUNNY. GREAT BIG BUILDINGS, CARS, HOT DOGS. YOU MUST HAVE SEEN A CITY BEFORE!
I... I DON'T REMEMBER.

THEY'RE COMING! WE MUST KEEP RUNNING! MEEP! RUNNING!
UH OH, DON'T LET HIM PICK UP SPEED IN HERE, OR...

RUNNING! ARGHHH!
PING!
PING!
VMMM!
PING!

TAKE THE PLANS! WE MIGHT NEED THEM!
I'M PANICKING!
I AM TAKING THEM! LET GO!
TUG!
MEEP!

FWOOM!
UH OH.
THE CANDLE!
PING!

IF YOU'RE GOING TO HAVE ANY CHANCE STOPPING THE HUMANS, YOU'RE GOING TO NEED TO BE BETTER THAN THIS.

I'LL LET YOU KNOW IF I HEAR ANY MORE.

"THE PURPLE!"

IT'S... BEAUTIFUL!

THE SATURN PURPLE, ONE OF THE RAREST FLOWERS IN THESE WOODS. THEY SAY WHEN IT BLOOMS, YOU CAN HEAR ANGELS SINGING!

HMPH!

WELL, I THINK IT'S DISGUSTING. LOOK AT IT, ALL PRETTY AND COLOURFUL.
UGH!

WHEN I OWN THE WOODS, I WILL BAN ALL NICE COLOURS.

THE BEST THING ABOUT THE SATURN BURPLE IS THAT YOU CAN PICK ITS SEEDS OFF...

...AND THEY SPLAT!
EEEEEE!
LIKE BURPLE PAINT!
TWANG!
SPLAT!
PURPLE.

GET AWAY FROM ME! I WILL NOT BE TAINTED WITH THIS RANCID... PURPLE!
BURPLE!
NO. PURPLE.

C'MON, MONKEY, IT'S FUN! IT'S LIKE PLAYING PAINTBALL!
SPLAT!
NO! NOOO!! ARGHHH!

SHRIIIEK!
GET IT AWAY FROM MEEEE!
HA HA HA! CHASE MONKEY!
SPLAT!
SPLAT!
YOU'RE FOULING EVERYTHING WITH IT!
SPLAT!
SPLAT!
IT'S THE PURPLE-OCALYPSE!
I CANNOT LIVE HERE, NOT NOW YOU'VE PAINTED THE WOODS PURPLE!
BURPLE.
PURPLE.
I'M ONLY RELIEVED YOU DIDN'T GET ANY ON ME.
SPLAT!
HA HA! NOW YOU'RE PLAYING TOO!
EEE HEE HEE! HEE HEE!
SNORT!
WAIT, IS HE CRYING OR LAUGHING?
I DON'T KNOW. I CAN'T TELL THE DIFFERENCE.

LAUGHING, YOU IDIOTS! I ACTUALLY LOVE THE COLOUR PURPLE, IT DOESN'T BOTHER ME AT ALL!
BUT NOW YOU'VE COVERED THE WOODS IN IT...
...LOOK AT ALL THE GLORIOUS MESS YOU'VE MADE!
WAIT.
WHAT?
BURPLE?
IT IS PURPLE! WITH A 'P'! PURPLE! PURPLE!!
HANG ON, DID MONKEY TRICK US?
DON'T THINK ABOUT IT, JUST KEEP SCRUBBING.
MEH HEH!
JAMIE

"THE WEIRD WOODS!"

-PART ONE-

ON THE EDGE OF THE WOODS THERE IS A MYSTERIOUS CABIN...

MYSTERIOUS, BECAUSE IT HOLDS ALL THE WOODS' MYSTERIES.

NOW.
WHERE WERE WE?
THE WEIRD WOODS WALL
AND ONE MAN IS DETERMINED TO FIGURE THEM OUT.

PHEW! SURE IS DARK OUT THERE, FELT LIKE SOMETHING WAS WATCHING ME, TOO.
PROBABLY WAS!
YOU'RE NOT LOOKING AT YOUR WEIRD WOODS WALL AGAIN, ARE YOU? LET IT GO.
BUT THERE ARE TOO MANY STRANGE THINGS GOING ON!

MASSIVE EXPLOSIONS! CLANKING MACHINERY! DISTANT GIGGLING, MANIACAL LAUGHING AND LOUD SCREAMING!
NOT TO MENTION THE THINGS WE'VE FOUND.
THAT GIANT EYEBALL EMBEDDED IN THE MIDDLE OF THE ROAD!

THE WEIRD, SPIKY, SKIN THAT BLEW INTO TOWN.

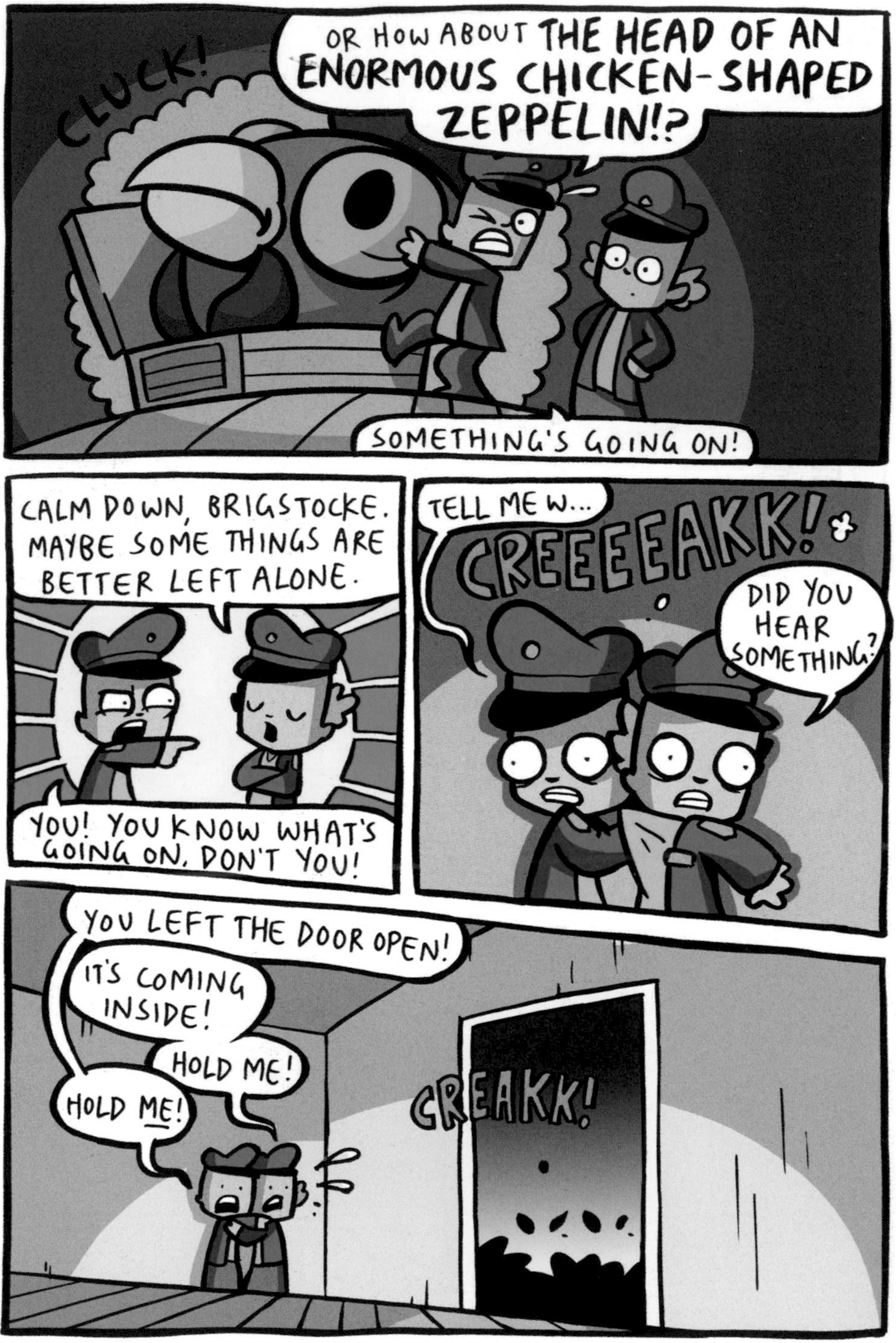

CALM DOWN, BRIGSTOCKE. MAYBE SOME THINGS ARE BETTER LEFT ALONE.

YOU! YOU KNOW WHAT'S GOING ON, DON'T YOU!

TELL ME W...

CREEEEAKK!

DID YOU HEAR SOMETHING?

YOU LEFT THE DOOR OPEN!

IT'S COMING INSIDE!

HOLD ME!

HOLD ME!

CREAKK!

WE'RE RAIDING YOUR FORT!! BLOO BLOO BLOO BLOO!!
BLOO.
SCREAM!
SCREAM!
PERHAPS SOME MYSTERIES WILL NEVER BE ANSWERED...
WHY WAS THAT PIG DRESSED LIKE THAT?

"THE WEIRD WOODS!"

-PART TWO-

IT'S THE MIDDLE OF THE NIGHT, AND CRASHING THROUGH THE WOODS COME WEENIE AND PIG, PURSUED BY...

BLOO BLOO BLOO!

HUUUUMANS!

AH'M **BUNNY THE KID**, AND YOU, OUTLAW PIG, ARE ABOUT TO GET A TASTE OF WILD WEST JUSTICE!

POK!

YEEE-HAW!

THEY'RE... FIRING AT US!

SHRIEK!

I THOUGHT WE WERE PLAYING COWBOYS AND ROBBERS!!
WE WERE...
BUT THEN HUMANS STARTED CHASING US!

THE HUMANS? COMING INTO OUR WOODS?
ZUT ALORS! ZE PROPHECY IS FINALLY COMING TRUE!

I MUST DESTROY MY NETWORK OF TUNNELS, ELSE THEY GET HOLD OF MY SECRETS!
TNT

PUFF PUFF! I CAN'T KEEP UP, BRIGSTOCKE! YOU... YOU GO ON WITHOUT ME!
I WILL! THIS MAY BE OUR BEST CHANCE TO DISCOVER WHAT GOES ON IN THESE WOODS!

ACTION BEAVER! THIS IS THE MISSION YOU'VE BEEN TRAINING FOR!
ARE YOU READY?
SCHHHP!

BOOM!
I'D CALL THAT A 'YES'.
GO, ACTION BEAVER! DEFEND OUR WOODS FROM THE INVADERS!

CLONK!
ARGH!

I AM DESTROYING IT ALL, HUMAN!
BOOM!
?!

BOOM!
BOOM!
WHAT...
...WHAT'S GOING ON?
CRAWL!

HAR HAR! EVERYONE SEEMS TO BE OUT, SO I HALF-INCHED ALL OF WEENIE'S FRESHLY BAKED BUNS!
CHOMP!
RUSTLE!

PLEASE DON'T TAKE MY BUNS!

THIS PLACE IS INSANE! I CAN'T TAKE IT!

SCREAM!
SCREAM!
THAT WAS THE HUMAN INVASION?
I BLEW EVERYTHING UP FOR NOTHING.
JAMIE

SUMMER

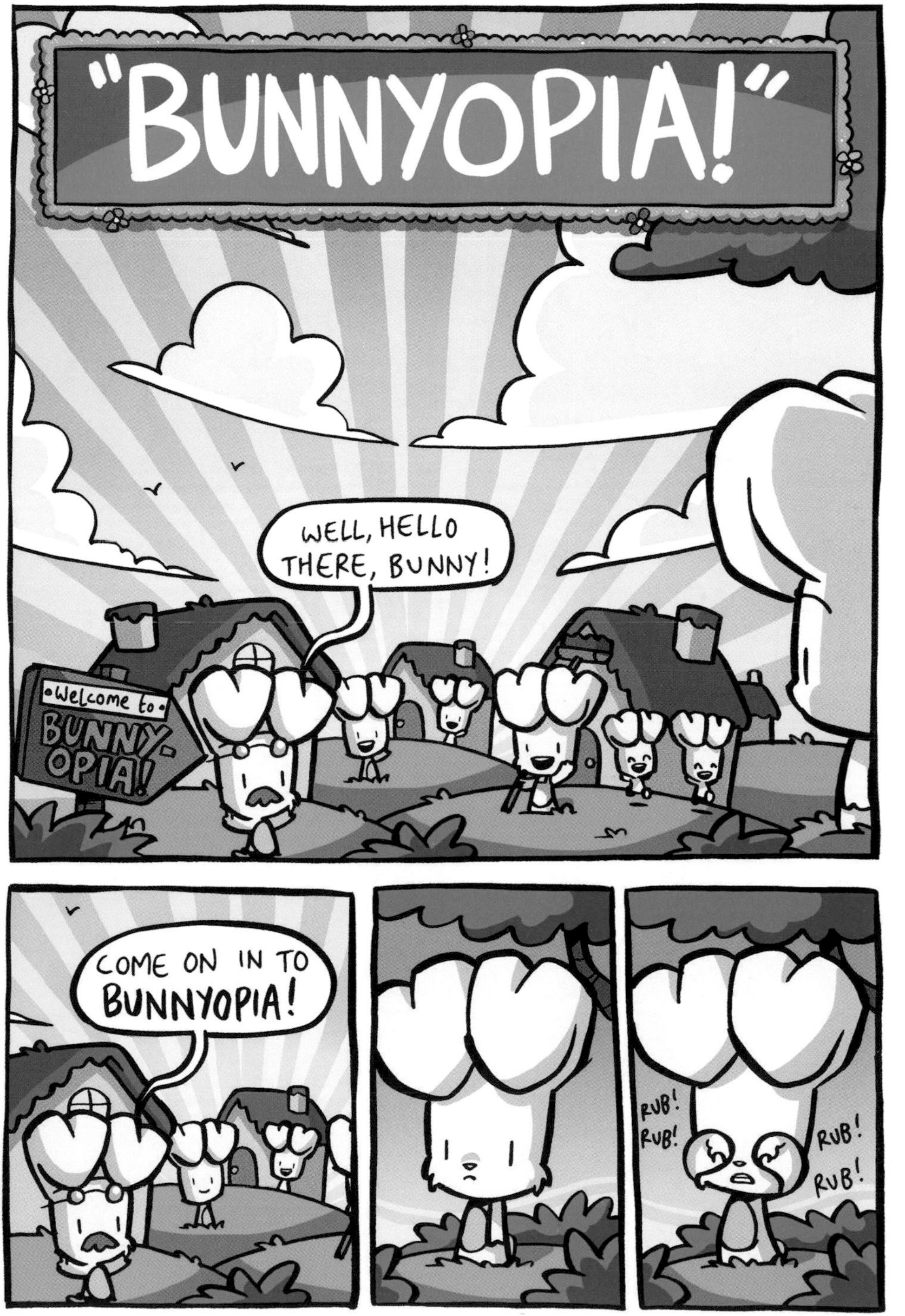

"BUNNYOPIA!"

WELL, HELLO THERE, BUNNY!

•Welcome to•
BUNNY-OPIA!

WHAT'S WRONG? WE BEEN WAITIN' FOR YOU!
I THOUGHT THIS MIGHT BE A CHEESE DREAM.

I'VE NOT REALLY MET MANY OTHER BUNNIES BEFORE. I HAD NO IDEA THIS WAS HERE.

I JUST HAD THIS MYSTERIOUS INVITATION PUSHED UNDER MY DOOR AND, WELL, HERE YOU ALL ARE!
COME TO BUNNYOPIA!
SHOOF!
WOULD YOU LIKE SOME **CARROT?**
I DON'T REALLY LIKE CARROTS.
YOU LOVE CARROTS. YOU JUST FORGOT.
HEE HEE.

NO REALLY, I... HANG ON, WHY DO YOU HAVE A **KEY** IN YOUR BACK?
WHY DO YOU ALL HAVE KEYS IN YOUR BACKS?

BZZT. CARROTS.
AND THESE 'HOUSES' AREN'T HOUSES AT ALL!

YOU'RE ROBOTS! BUNNYOPIA ISN'T REAL!
BZZT! SUBJECT HAS REALISED DECEPTION.

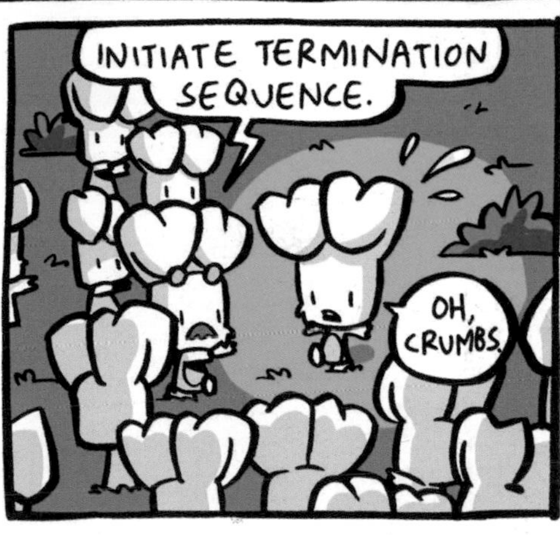
INITIATE TERMINATION SEQUENCE.
OH, CRUMBS.

EEEEEEEEE!

BUNNY! YOU'RE MEANT TO BE IN BUNNYOPIA!
WHAT? HOW DO YOU KNOW ABOUT BUNNYOPIA?

WHY WOULD YOU...
SIGH... I BUILT BUNNYOPIA SO YOU MIGHT GO AND LIVE THERE, WHILE MONKEY AND I FIRE YOUR HOUSE INTO SPACE!
BUT YOU'VE RUINED THE SURPRISE!

ACTUALLY, NEVER MIND. JUST USE YOUR ROCKET TO SAVE US ALL FROM BUNNYOCALYPSE!
ULP!

BZZT.
WELCOME TO BUNNYOPIA!
HAVE A CUSHION.
BZZT!
JAMIE

I THOUGHT, FOR A MOMENT, I MIGHT ACTUALLY HAVE ...A FAMILY.
BZZT. CARROTS.

WOOOSH!
IF ANYONE NEEDS ME, I'LL BE ON MY OWN.
AGAIN.

IN SPACE...
CARROTS.
UM, GROUND CONTROL?
BZZT.
WERE THERE ALWAYS BUNNIES UP HERE?

"OCTO-FOX!"

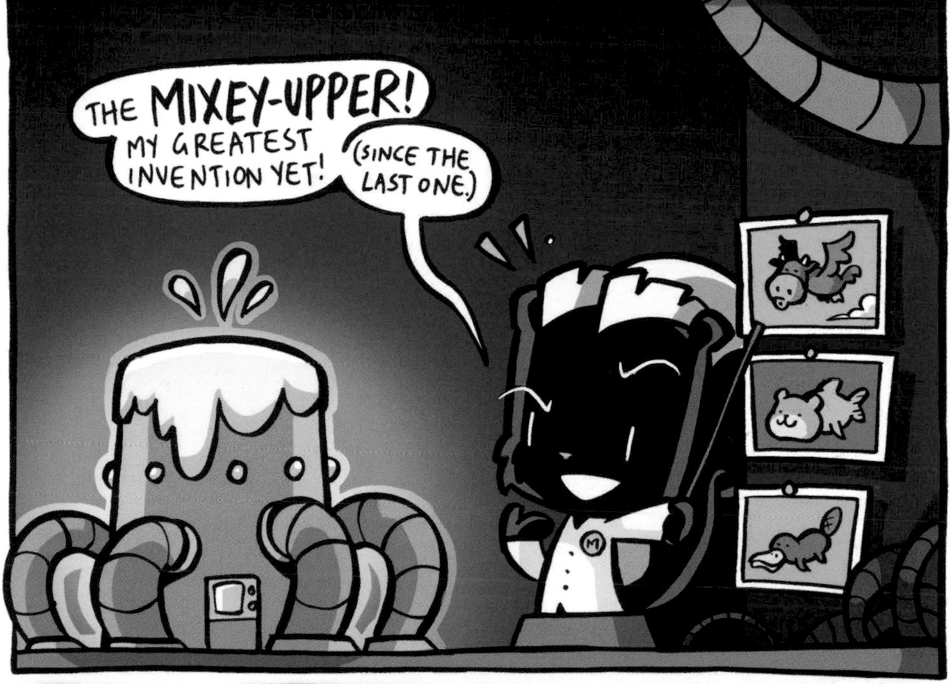

THE MIXEY-UPPER! MY GREATEST INVENTION YET!
(SINCE THE LAST ONE.)

I'M READY! CAN I GET IN NOW?
HOLD ON, MONKEY! FIRST WE HAVE TO PROGRAM WHICH ANIMAL WE MIX YOU WITH!

ALL OF THEM!
SKK!
UH?

SO! ZIS IS WHERE YOU DESPICABLE FIENDS HIDE OUT, RIGHT BENEATH MY TUNNELS!
CRACK!
LE FOX!
HANG ON, WHAT'S...

SPLOSH!
EUGH!
NO! GET OUT OF THE MIXEY-UPPER!

FZZT! BANG!
ARGH! HE'S SHORT-CIRCUITED THE CONTROLS!

HE COULD BE MIXING WITH ANYTHING.
BLOOP! GLOOP!

ZUT.

A TERRIFYING **OCTO-FOX**!
HE STOLE MY CHANCE! THAT COULD HAVE BEEN ME!

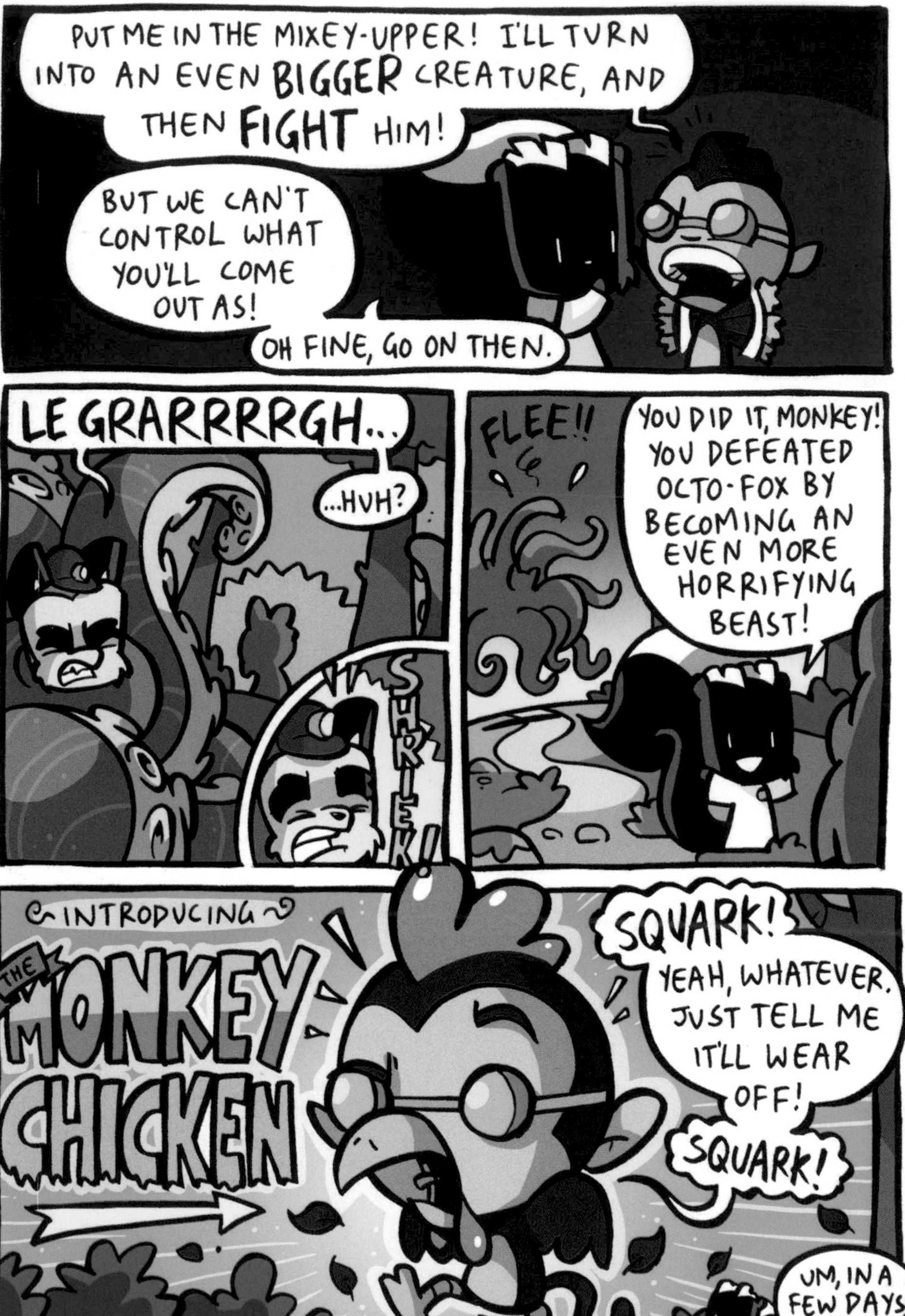

LE GRARRRRGH...
...HUH?
SHRIEK!
FLEE!!
YOU DID IT, MONKEY! YOU DEFEATED OCTO-FOX BY BECOMING AN EVEN MORE HORRIFYING BEAST!
~INTRODUCING~
THE MONKEY CHICKEN
SQUARK!
YEAH, WHATEVER. JUST TELL ME IT'LL WEAR OFF!
SQUARK!
UM, IN A FEW DAYS, SURE. MAYBE.
JAMIE

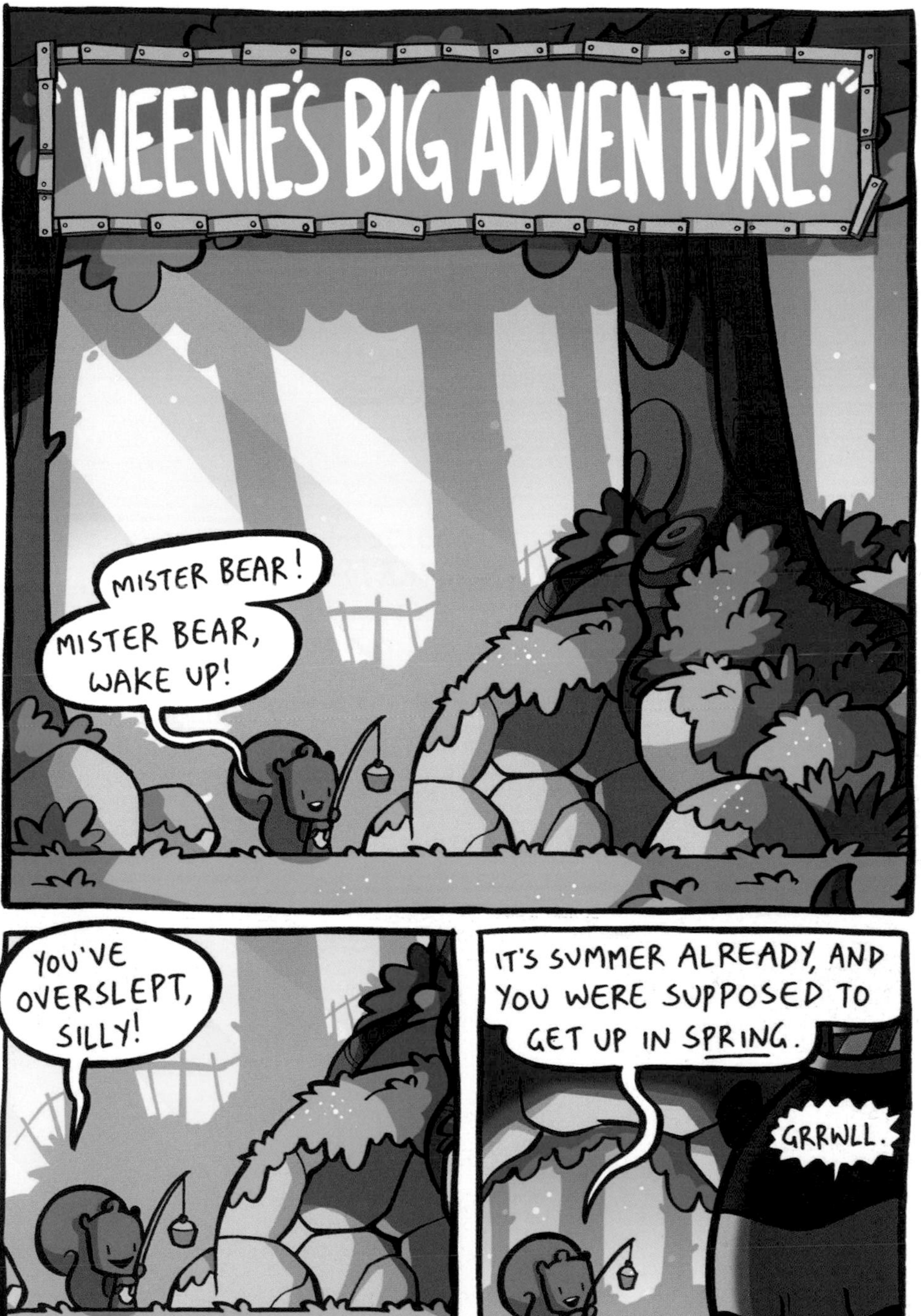

"WEENIE'S BIG ADVENTURE!"

MISTER BEAR!

MISTER BEAR, WAKE UP!

I CAME TO ASK IF YOU'D LIKE TO JOIN ME ON A BIG ADVENTURE! EVERYONE ELSE IN THE WOODS IS BUSY, FIGHTING WITH EACH OTHER, BUT IT'S TOO BEAUTIFUL A DAY TO WASTE!

I THINK WE'VE DONE EVERYTHING THERE IS TO DO ON EARTH TODAY, MISTER BEAR!
BUT THERE'S ONE PLACE LEFT WE HAVEN'T BEEN!

WHEEEEEHEEEE!!
PLUH!
HERE I COME, THE MOON!

CLONK!
OW!
HEE HEE!
FELL A BIT SHORT.
LET'S GO AGAIN!

OKAY, THIS TIME, WE NEED MORE UP.
WEENIE?

WEENIE'S BEING EATEN BY THE BEAR!!
UH OH.

RUN, MISTER BEAR! WE'RE IN TROUBLE NOW!
GET AWAY FROM HIM!
RRF! RRF!

SOMETIME LATER...
IT'S BEEN A WHILE SINCE BUNNY STOPPED SEARCHING FOR US, AND I'M GETTING TIRED.
MAYBE WE SHOULD GO TO SLEEP NOW.

BECAUSE SOME DAYS ARE WORTH DREAMING ABOUT...
...ALL OVER AGAIN.

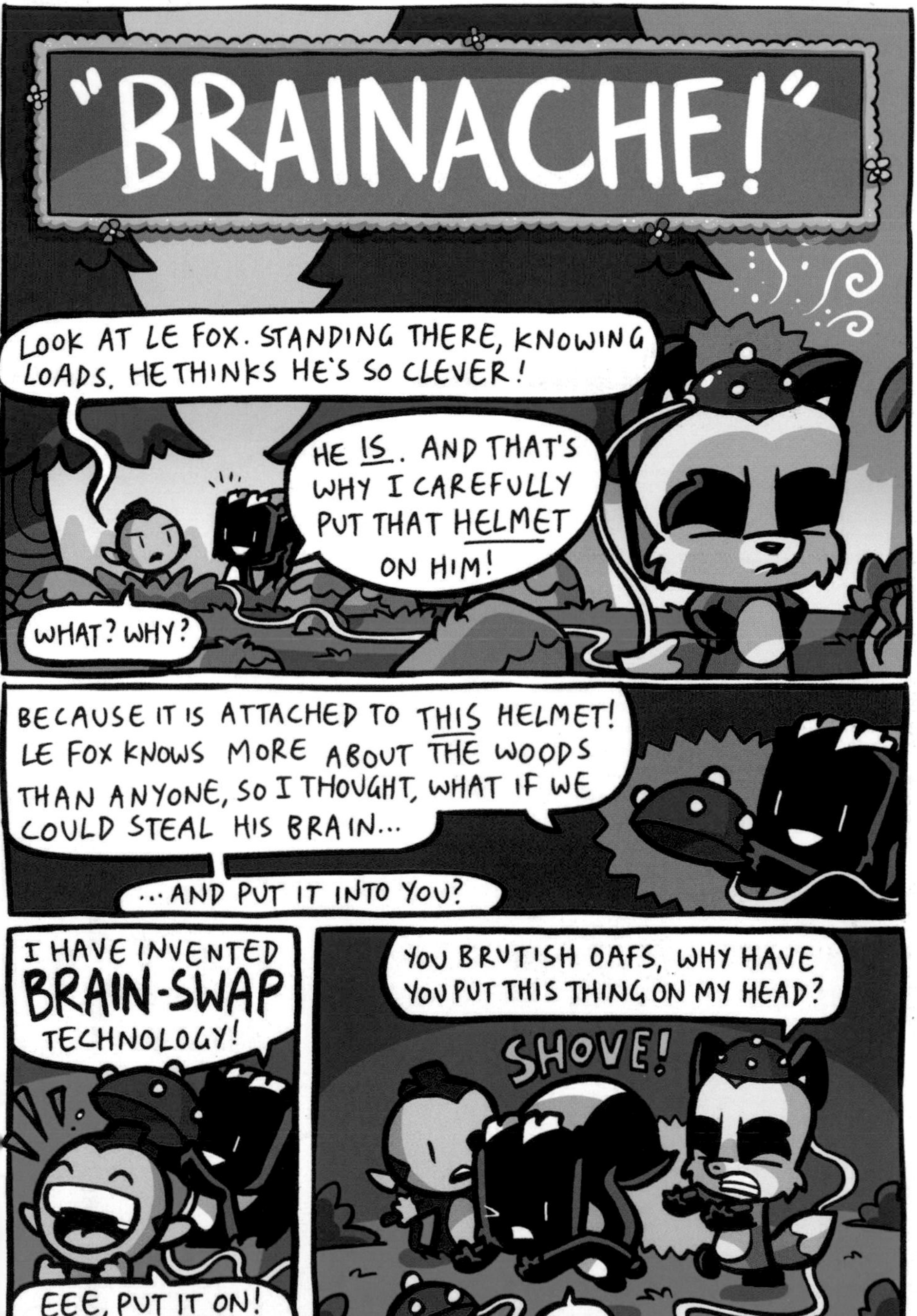

"BRAINACHE!"

LOOK AT LE FOX. STANDING THERE, KNOWING LOADS. HE THINKS HE'S SO CLEVER!

HE IS. AND THAT'S WHY I CAREFULLY PUT THAT HELMET ON HIM!

WHAT? WHY?

BECAUSE IT IS ATTACHED TO THIS HELMET! LE FOX KNOWS MORE ABOUT THE WOODS THAN ANYONE, SO I THOUGHT, WHAT IF WE COULD STEAL HIS BRAIN...

...AND PUT IT INTO YOU?

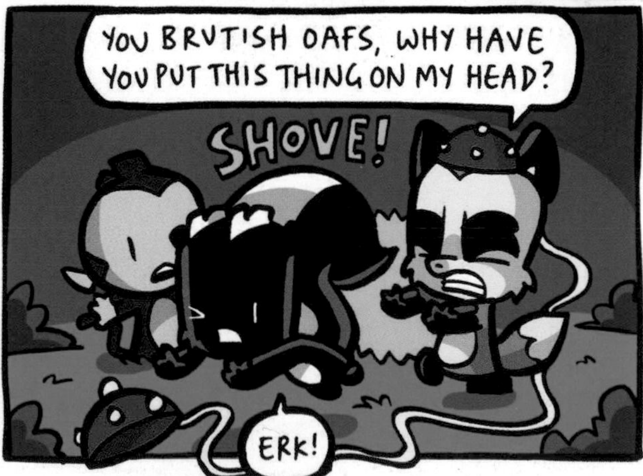

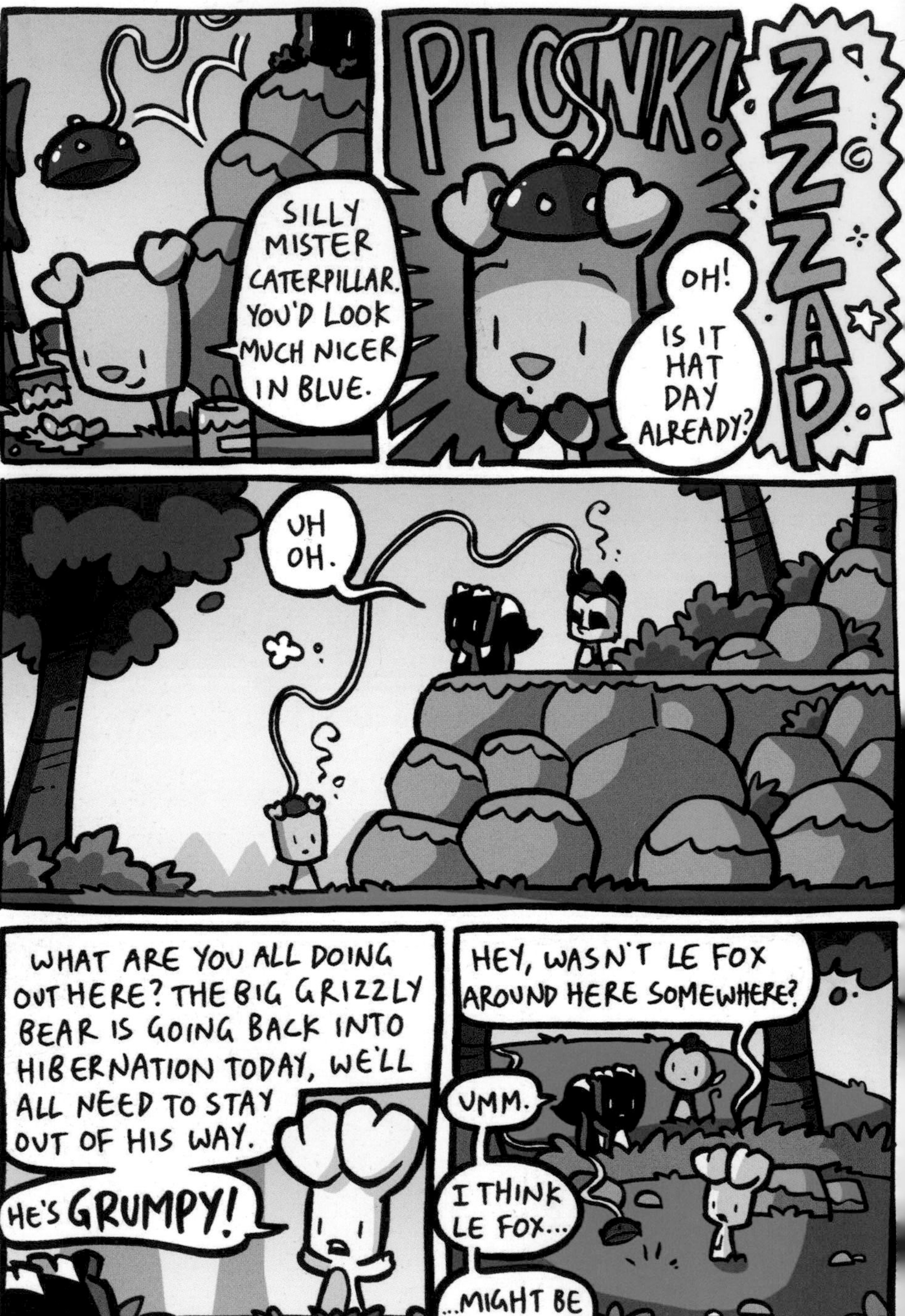

SILLY MISTER CATERPILLAR. YOU'D LOOK MUCH NICER IN BLUE.

PLONK!

ZZZAP

OH!

IS IT HAT DAY ALREADY?

UH OH.

WHEE
EEEE
EEEE
EEEE
EEE!!

THAT'S FUNNY. I DON'T REMEMBER HAVING A BIG TAIL.
OR FUR.
OR A FRENCH ACCENT.

OR STANDING NEXT TO A BEAR.
GRRRWLL!

POKE!
POKE!

SHRIIIIEK! THERE'S A BIG BEAR CHASING ME FOR NO REASON I CAN REMEMBER!
AARGH!

RRR

PLONK!
URF!
TAKE ZAT, YOU UNRULY FURBALL!
ZZZAP

HOORAY! PIG... I MEAN, LE FOX, SAVED US!
UM.
WAIT, WHO'S IN WHICH BODY NOW?

IT'S ABOUT TIME YOU TWO HAD A BEAR HUG!
SCREAM! LE FOX! I KNOW THAT'S YOU!
COME ON PIG, TIME TO GO BACK TO HIBERNATION.
GRRWLL.
HEE HEE!
SANIE

"WOODLAND STORY!"

PIG GOT HIS HEAD STUCK IN A BEACHBALL!

WE'RE NOT QUITE SURE HOW.

THAT'S DEFINITELY GOING INTO MY BOOK.
OOH, YOU'RE WRITING A BOOK?
CAN IT BE ABOUT DINOSAURS?
SCRIBBLE!

NO. IT'S GOING TO BE A COMPREHENSIVE HISTORY OF THE WOODS! AN ACCOUNT OF ALL THE MAD THINGS THAT HAPPEN, AS WELL AS THE STORY OF WHERE WE ALL CAME FROM!

WELL, THAT'S EASY. I WAS MADE FROM FLOUR, EGGS, ICING SUGAR, SWEETNESS AND CUDDLES!
MY MUMMY SAID SO.

UM, I DON'T THINK SHE MEANT IT LITERALLY, WEENIE.
DID.
I CAME FROM FARRR AWAYYY.

A GIANT BUTTERFLY BROUGHT ME TO THE WOODS.
AND IT TOLD ME THAT ONE DAY IT WOULD COME BACK FOR ME!
FLAP! FLAP!

RIIIIIGHT. YOU TWO AREN'T BEING MUCH HELP.
CAN WE STILL BE IN THE BOOK?
CAN I BE A DINOSAUR?
RARR!

PSST! I HEAR YOU ARE WRITING A BOOK ABOUT US.
THAT'S RIGHT, LE FOX. I'M GUESSING YOU WON'T TELL ME ANYTHING THOUGH.

ALL I WILL TELL YOU IS STAY AWAY. STAY AWAY FROM OUR SECRETS. STAY AWAY FROM THE TRUTH. FOR YOU MAY NOT LIKE WHAT YOU FIND.
I AM IN DISGUISE, BY THE WAY.

OKAY, WHATEVER.
THANKS.
STAYYY AWAYYY!

WELL, IIII WAS SENT TO YOUR PLANET BY THE PEOPLE OF EARTH, DESTINED TO BECOME A CONQUEROR OF YOUR WORLD!

MONK OPIA!

HRGH!

ARE YOU... ARE YOU FALLING ASLEEP IN FRONT OF YOUR GLORIOUS LEADER?

ZZZ.

BANG!

EEE!

THIS IS MY NEWEST INVENTION, THE BANGBANG!
IT GOES BANG.
THAT'S ABOUT IT.
AS FOR MY STORY.

I USED TO LIVE IN THE CITY, SCAVENGING FOOD LIKE A COMMON ANIMAL. BUT THEN I DISCOVERED SCIENCE, AND FLEW TO THE WOODS SO I COULD CONTINUE MY RESEARCH IN PEACE!
WOOSH!
WOOOSHH!

OH, THIS IS USELESS! ALL YOUR STORIES ARE RIDICULOUS, NO ONE WILL BELIEVE ANY OF THIS!
RIP!
RIP!
RIP!
RIP!
RIP!
RIIIIIP!
RIP!
RIP!
RIP!
RIP!

WHAT ABOUT YOU, BUNNY? HOW DID YOU GET HERE?
THAT'S JUST IT...

I DON'T REMEMBER HOW I GOT HERE! I THOUGHT BY WRITING ABOUT YOUR PASTS, I MIGHT REMEMBER MY OWN.
MAYBE IT DOESN'T MATTER WHERE WE COME FROM.
JAMIE

WHAT MATTERS IS WHERE WE ARE NOW.
AND WHERE WE ARE NOW...

...IS MONKEYOPIA!
SIGHH.
NOT MONKEY-OPIA.
BWOO HAR HAR HARRR!
IS MONKEYOPIA.

"SO MANY MONKEYS!"

SKUNKY, I HAD A TERRIBLE DREAM LAST NIGHT. IT WAS AWFUL!
DID BANANAS GROW OUT OF YOUR NOSE?
I HAVE THAT DREAM SOMETIMES TOO.
SHUDDER!

WHAT? NO! I DREAMT THAT I FINALLY ACHIEVED MONKEY-O-PIA, THEN DIED BEFORE I COULD ENJOY IT!
I CAN'T DIE!
AHH. MORTALITY.

IT IS THE CYCLE OF LIFE, MONKEY. ALL THINGS IN NATURE GROW, BLOSSOM, THEN WITHER...
NONSENSE! I WANT YOU TO CLONE ME!

CLONE ME! MAKE A SPARE ME, SO WE HAVE A BACK-UP MONKEY.
WE NEED A BACK-UP MONKEY!

A FEW HOURS LATER...
SO, THE CLONE-A-TRON DEVICE SHOULD EXTRACT YOUR DNA, AND SYNTHESISE IT EXACTLY...
YEAH YEAH! PUSH THE BUTTON!

BZZZZ!!
IT'S ME!
IT'S YOU!
THAT IS AMAZING, SKUNKY. A SPARE ME, TO CARRY ON MY WORK!
I MEANT YOU.
YOU ARE!
NOW, HANG ON, ME? I'M THE NEWER VERSION, IT'S OBVIOUS I SHOULD BE MONKEY NOW.
BUT I'M THE ORIGINAL!
YOU'LL GET IN THE WAY OF ME TAKING OVER THE WOODS!
YOU'LL GET IN THE WAY OF ME TAKING OVER THE WOODS.
SO WHICH ONE OF US IS THE ORIGINAL? WE NEED A THIRD OPINION!
AGREED! ANOTHER MONKEY WILL SOLVE THIS.

BZZZZZ!!!
IT'S ME!
IT'S YOU!
IT'S US!
MONKEY, WHICH MONKEY SHOULD BE IN CHARGE?
WELL, ME! I AM MONKEY, AFTER ALL!
SIGHHH. LET'S TRY AGAIN.
WITHIN MINUTES...
I'M BEGINNING TO THINK THIS WAS A BAD IDEA.

"A NEW CHALLENGER APPEARS!"

HEE HEE! YOU'LL NEVER HIT ME WITH YOUR PEA-SHOOTER!
OW!

SIGH. I CAME TO THIS PART OF THE WOODS FOR SOME PEACE.

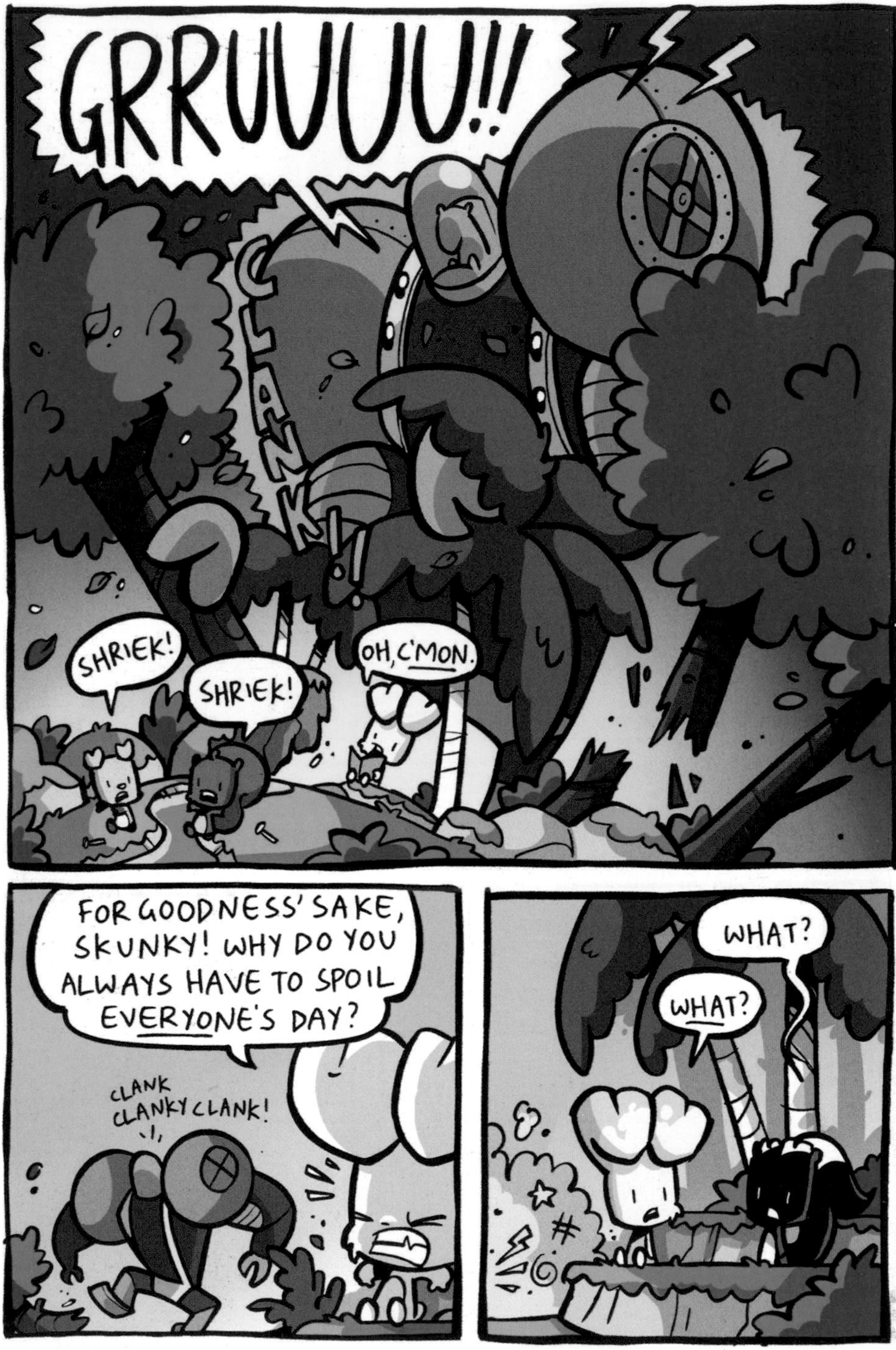

GRRUUUU!!
CLANK!
SHRIEK!
SHRIEK!
OH, C'MON.

THEN WHO...?
HAR HAR! I AM THE MANIACAL BADGER, CAUSING HAVOC WITH MY TERRIFYING CREATURES!

GASP! ANOTHER GENIUS INVENTOR IN THE WOODS?
ANOTHER? YOU MEAN THE ONLY!

NAH. I AM SKUNKY, THE MOST BRILLIANT MIND IN THE ANIMAL KINGDOM!
NO! I WILL NOT HAVE MY BRILLIANCE BETTERED!

YOU FOUND A WAY INTO MY LAIR, THAT'S ALL. NO ONE CAN RIVAL MY SUPERIOR EVIL BRAIN!
THEN TELL ME, HAVE YOU EVER...

...INVENTED A PORTABLE ROCKET SEAT, CAPABLE OF REACHING THE STRATOSPHERE?
FWOOOOM!
NO, I HAVEN'T.

FWOOSH
MINE CAN REACH THE MOON!!
HOW ABOUT... A DONKEY SUIT WHICH FIRES LASERS FROM ITS NOSTRILS?
BZZT!
BOOM!
OH, I PUT A HAT ON MINE.
A CTHULHU...
...MADE OF JELLY!
BZZT!
A GIANT...
...MADE OF GRANITE!
BOP!
?
THAT...
IS...
ENOUGH!

BOTH OF YOU, STOP IT. YOU'RE JUST SHOWING-OFF IN FRONT OF EACH OTHER.

SORRY, BUNNY.
SORRY, BUNNY.

HERE, IF YOU REALLY HAVE TO FIGHT, TAKE THESE PEA-SHOOTERS AND DO IT QUIETLY.

YES, BUNNY.
SORRY, BUNNY.

I WAS WINNING.
OW. I WAS WINNING.
PTOO!
NO!

SORRY, BUNNY.
SORRY, BUNNY.

"SEE-SAW!"

EMPLOYEES ONLY
WHAT IS THIS PLACE?

THIS IS MY ADVENTURE PLAYGROUND. I FOUND IT, SO IT IS MINE.
NO BUNNIES ALLOWED!

IT'S A BIT RUBBISH, THOUGH. EVERYTHING'S BROKEN.
WHAT HAPPENED HERE?

FIVE MINUTES EARLIER...
HAMMERHAMMER
ERHAMMER
MMERHAM
AMMER!
SMASH!

I DUNNO. IT'S A MYSTERY. WHAT ARE YOU DOING HERE?
I'VE BEEN OUT CLEANING UP DEER POO!
DEER POO
I DO WISH THEY'D PICK IT UP THEMSELVES.

WELL, YOU CAN GO NOW. YOU ARE NOT WORTHY TO COME AND PLAY IN MY TERRIBLE PLAYGROUND.
THERE MUST BE SOMETHING STILL IN ONE PIECE.

A SEE-SAW!
NOW THAT WAS BROKEN WHEN I GOT HERE.

IT'S NOT BROKEN, YOU IDIOT. IT JUST NEEDS TWO OF US TO WORK IT!
YOU SIT HERE.

AND I'LL SIT UP HERE.
HRRG!
NO NEED TO HELP.
'KAY.

THERE!
NOW WHAT? DOES IT EXPLODE?!

NO IT DOES NOT. WE GO UP AND DOWN, LIKE THIS!
WHEEE!

WHEE!

BORRRING. I'M GETTING OFF.
CLONK!

MONKEY, THE SEE-SAW REQUIRES TWO OF US WORKING TOGETHER. TRUSTING EACH OTHER.
MAYBE IT'S OUR CHANCE TO MAKE PEACE FOR ONCE.

THINKING...
MEH HEH HEH...
THINKING.

OKAY, BUNNY, I'M GETTING BACK ON...
...AND FIRING YOU INTO THE SKY!
LEAP!

DEER POO
WHIZZZ!
UH?
CLONK!

SPLUTCH!
ARGHH! DEER POO!

WHAT, DO YOU THINK I'M STUPID, MONKEY? AS IF I COULD TRUST YOU.
BOO HOO HOO!

"GRAV-O-BOX!"

I AM THE GREAT UNDERSEA EXPLORER JACQUES DE HONK HONK!
AND I AM A FISH!

I WILL NAME THIS FISH THE 'DE HONK HONK'... WHOAAA!
EEE!
WHIZZZZZ!

BUNNY, WEENIE JUST GOT PULLED UP THE WATERFALL!
NO HE DIDN'T, PIG. WATERFALLS DON'T RUN UP!

HE DID! HE DID! LET ME IN, I'M SCARED OF THE WATER!

PIG, IT'S BASIC PHYSICS. WATER FLOWS...

...UPPP!?!
EEK! WHAT'S GOING ON?
WHIZZZZZ!

MY LATEST BRILLIANT INVENTION, THE **GRAV-O-BOX**, COMPLETELY REDEFINES THE LAWS OF GRAVITY!

...AND I ACCIDENTALLY TURNED IT ON.

NOW I CAN'T GET CLOSE ENOUGH TO TURN IT OFF!

HELP ME, BUNNY! I'M GETTING SEASICK!
BUT...BUT YOU'RE A GREAT UNDERWATER EXPLORER!
HE'S RIGHT, WEENIE. NOW IS THE TIME FOR JACK HONKY HONK-HONK TO SAVE THE DAY!
YOU'RE RIGHT!
EXCEPT ABOUT MY NAME.
BLOOP!
THERE IT IS! HOW INCREDIBLE! I HAVE DISCOVERED IT ON MY FIRST DIVE!
WHIRRR!!

BUT HOW WOULD A GREAT UNDERWATER EXPLORER HANDLE SUCH A TREASURE?
SMASH IT WITH A ROCK!!
EEE!
TINKLE!
LUZZ!
SPLOSH!!
JAMIE
YOU DID IT, WEENIE! YOU'RE A GREAT UNDERWATER EXPLORER!
OHHH NO, I DON'T WANT TO BE ANY MORE.
WATER'S A BIT TOO WET FOR MY LIKING.

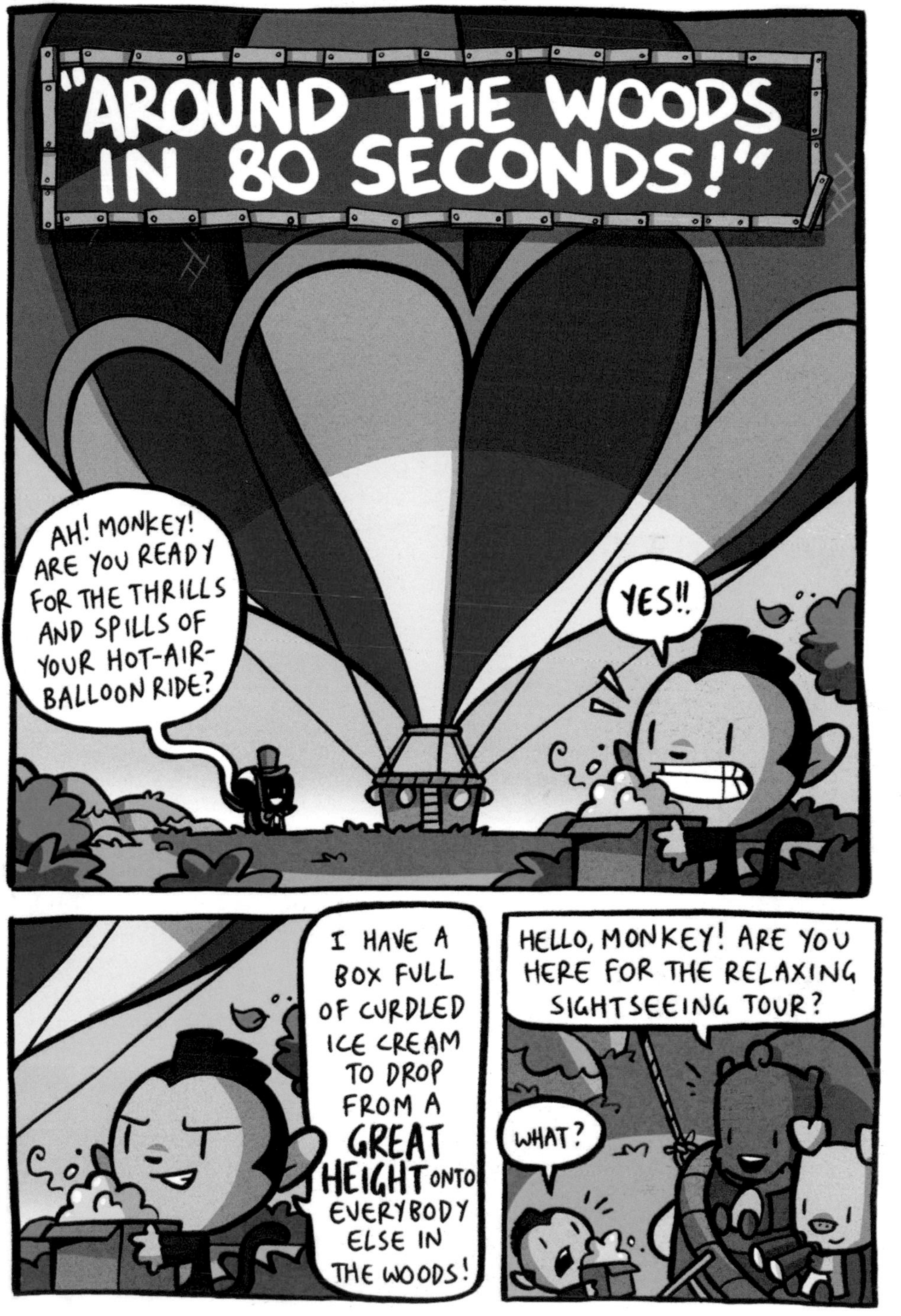

"AROUND THE WOODS IN 80 SECONDS!"

AH! MONKEY! ARE YOU READY FOR THE THRILLS AND SPILLS OF YOUR HOT-AIR-BALLOON RIDE?

YES!!

LISTEN, THEY PAID ME IN ICED BUNS TO SHOW THEM THE WOODS FROM THE AIR. YOU'LL STILL GET TO WREAK YOUR CURDLED HAVOC.
WELL.
I HOPE SO.

HAVOC? I THOUGHT THIS WAS MEANT TO BE FUN.
BUNNY TOO? WHO ELSE?

SHH! I AM A STOWAWAY!
SUPPLIES
OKAY. SORRY.

HANG ON. IF YOU'RE ALL IN HERE, THEN WHO AM I DROPPING ICE CREAM ON?

DON'T WORRY, MONKEY, WE'LL GET THEIR TOUR OUT OF THE WAY IN AN INSTANT WITH MY...
BOOP!

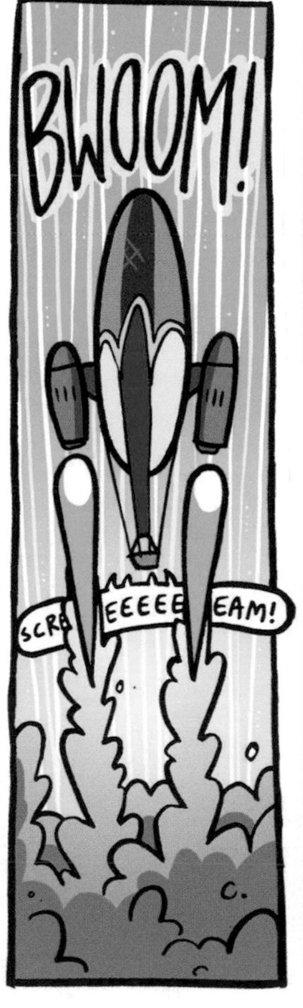

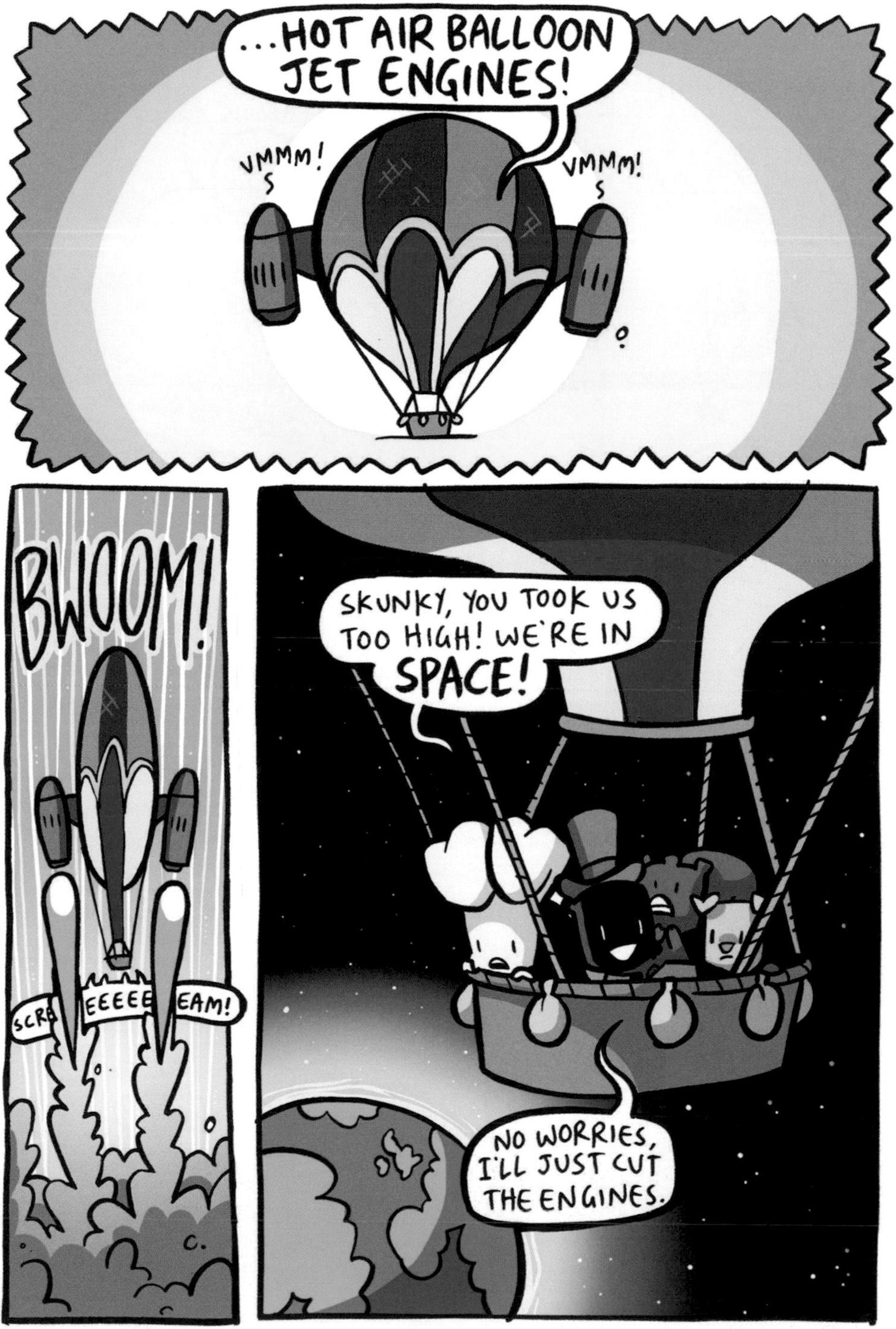

SKUNKY, YOU TOOK US TOO HIGH! WE'RE IN **SPACE!**

NO WORRIES, I'LL JUST CUT THE ENGINES.

THPTHBTHHH!
OH, HANG ON.
SKUNKY, YOU PROMISED US A TRANQUIL GUIDED TOUR, AND INSTEAD WE'RE FALLING TO OUR DOOM!
I CAN FIX THIS!
I CAN FIX THIS!
BOOP! BOOP!
PLUMMET!
PUTT! PUTT!
BWOOO
M!
THERE!
THE TOUR BEGINS NOW!
THERE'S THE ANGRY BEAR.
SCREEEAM!
UP HERE IS 'MILITARY ADVANTAGE PEAK'!
SCREEAM!

'THE HAUNTED STUMP'!
'DEVIL'S DROP'!
'SKUNKY'S CRATER'.
MONKEY, YOU MIGHT WANT TO THROW YOUR ICE CREAM NOW!
WHAT? ARGH!
WE'RE AT THE END OF OUR TOUR. NOW, THE INCREDIBLE LANDING!
EVERYONE, CLOSE YOUR EYES!
HUH?
CRASH!!
HOPE YOU ALL ENJOYED SKUNKY'S TOURS! Y'ALL TELL YOUR FRIENDS NOW!
I'M GOING TO BE SICK EVERY-WHERE!
BOO HOO HOO
I CAN SEE FEELINGS!
I'M SORRY FOR ALL THE BAD THINGS I'VE EVER DONE.
JAMIE

"FAT MONKEY"

AHH... THIS IS THE LIFE.

DAYDREAMING ABOUT FINALLY BECOMING A **GLORIOUS MONKEY EMPEROR**, WHILE MY STUPID MANSERVANT, WEENIE, FEEDS ME DELICIOUS LEMON DRIZZLE CAKES!

MONKEY? YOU LOOK... ENORMOUS!
THRRP!
HUH?

YES, WELL, IF THIS SQUIRREL WILL KEEP FEEDING ME HIS HOME-COOKED LEMON DRIZZLE CAKES!
YOU TOLD ME I'D WON A COMPETITION.

I REALLY THINK YOU SHOULD STOP EATING CAKES AND DO SOME EXERCISE, MONKEY.
NO ONE TELLS ME WHAT TO DO! I'M GOING TO COME OVER THERE AND...

OH, FORGET IT.
IT'S TOO TIRING TO MOVE.
WHEEZE!

I CAN'T SEIZE CONTROL OF THE WOODS WHILE I'M ALL FAT LIKE THIS! HELP ME GET BACK INTO SHAPE, BUNNY!
NO WAY! YOU'RE FAR LESS DANGEROUS LIKE THIS!

EITHER YOU HELP ME SHAPE UP, OR I'M EATING ALL WEENIE'S LEMON DRIZZLE CAKES!
NOOOOO! THEY'RE FOR MY HIBERNATION!
SNATCH!

SIGH.
FINE.

PUFF! PUFF!

GLUB GLUB!

DOOF DOOF!

A LITTLE WHILE LATER...
I DID IT! I HAVE RETURNED TO MY ORIGINAL TONED PHYSIQUE!
I AM A MONKEY ADONIS!

GOOD. NOW GIVE WEENIE HIS CAKES BACK.
HA HA HA HA.
NOPE.

IF I AM EVER GOING TO BE GLORIOUS MONKEY EMPEROR, THEN I MUST ALWAYS BE AS CRUEL AS POSSIBLE!
CHOMP! CHOMP!
HAR HAR NOM!

FWRRRP!
!!

AARGH, I GOT ALL FAT AGAIN! CURSE MY MONKEY METABOLISM!
YOU JUST UNDID ALL YOUR HARD WORK BY BEING SPITEFUL.
GOOD.

AM I GOING TO STARVE THIS WINTER, BUNNY?
HANG ON, WEENIE, YOU DON'T EVEN HIBERNATE.
OH.
OH YEAH.
BOO HOO HOO
YAY YYY YYY!

EPILOGUE!
GENTLEMEN, DO YOU REMEMBER WHEN WE HERE AT THE BRITISH SPACE PROGRAMME FIRED A MONKEY INTO SPACE?
VAAAGUELY.

WELL, WE PICKED UP A CURIOUS TRACKING SIGNAL.
AND WE FOUND HIM. RIGHT HERE ON EARTH.

GOOD GRIEF, CAN'T HAVE BEEN HARD TO SPOT HIM.
IS HE...IS HE CRYING?
IT DOESN'T MATTER.

THAT IS OUR MONKEY...
...AND WE MUST GET HIM BACK.

"MONKEY AT WORK!"

AHH, WHAT A BEAUTIFUL SUMMER MORNING...
HANG ON.
HAVE I ALWAYS LIVED BY THE RAVINE?

MONKEY! WHAT ARE YOU DOING?
I'M HELPING YOU MOVE HOUSE!
BRUM!

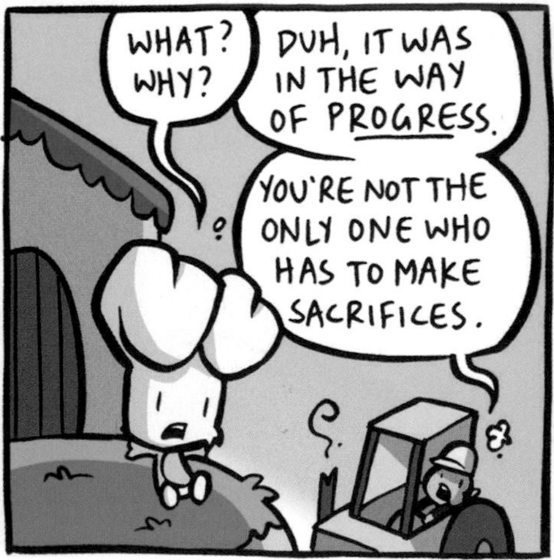

WHAT? WHY?
DUH, IT WAS IN THE WAY OF PROGRESS.
YOU'RE NOT THE ONLY ONE WHO HAS TO MAKE SACRIFICES.

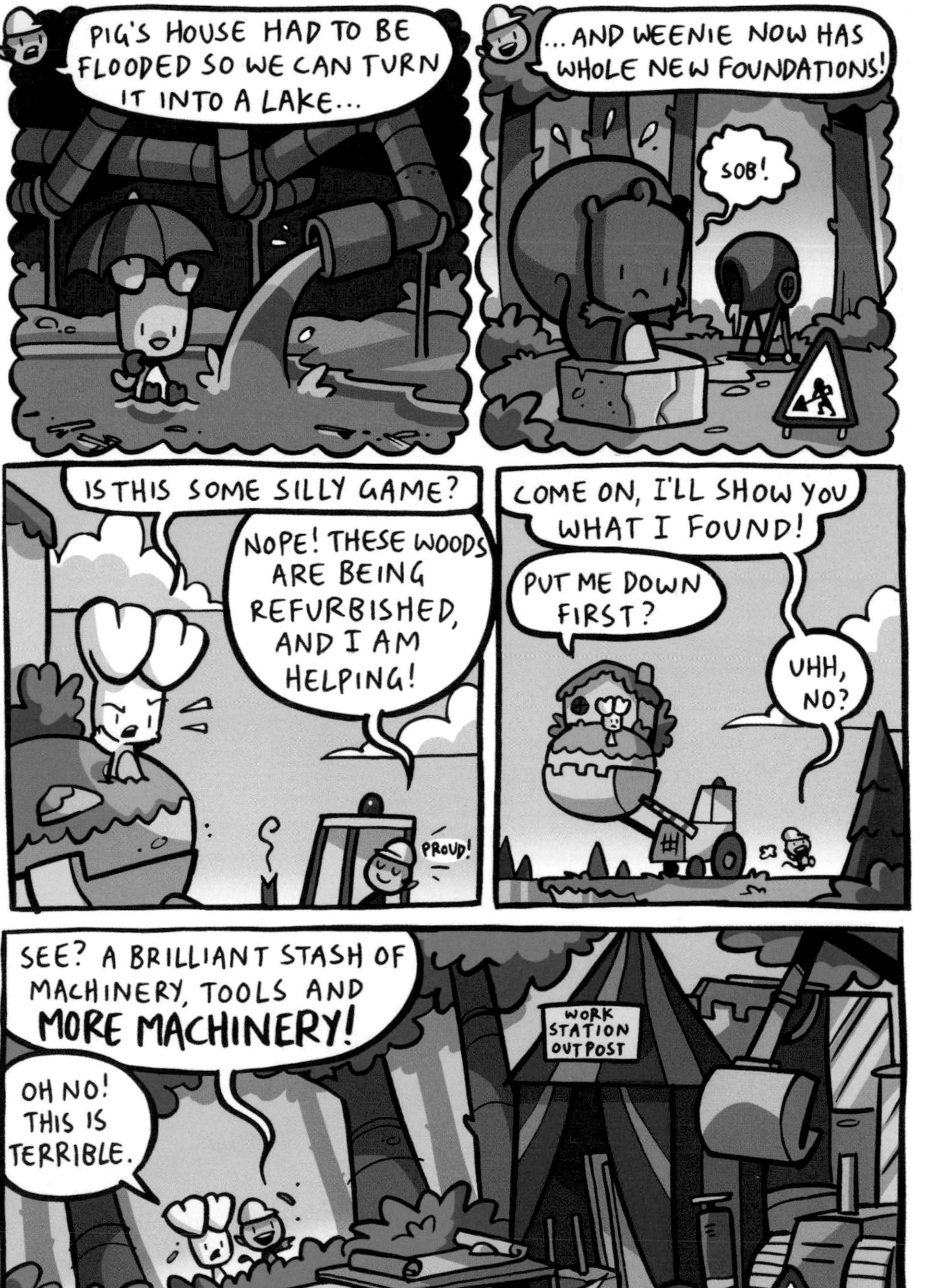

PIG'S HOUSE HAD TO BE FLOODED SO WE CAN TURN IT INTO A LAKE...

...AND WEENIE NOW HAS WHOLE NEW FOUNDATIONS!

SOB!

IS THIS SOME SILLY GAME?

NOPE! THESE WOODS ARE BEING REFURBISHED, AND I AM HELPING!

PROUD!

COME ON, I'LL SHOW YOU WHAT I FOUND!

PUT ME DOWN FIRST?

UHH, NO?

MACHINERY, BUNNY. CAN YOU IMAGINE MY FACE?!!
SO!
HAPPY!

THE HUMANS MUST BE CLOSER THAN WE THOUGHT. REMEMBER THE HUMANS, MONKEY? THEY WANT TO BUILD A ROAD THROUGH OUR WOODS.

I KNOW! I'VE SEEN THEIR PLANS!

IT LOOKS BUHH-RILLIANT.

EEK, THEY'RE COMING BACK!
HIDE!
WHEE!
SCARPER!

I STILL DON'T GET IT, CLAUDE. ONE OF OUR DIGGERS IS DEFINITELY MISSING.

THAT WAS ME!

MMF!

MONKEY, WE HAVE TO MAKE THEM LEAVE!
NO! THEY ARE MY FRIENDS.

FINE. IF YOU WON'T HELP, THEN IT'S UP TO THE REST OF US. I'M TIRED OF RUNNING AND HIDING WHENEVER HUMANS COME INTO OUR WOODS.
IT'S ABOUT TIME WE MADE A STAND, TO USE THE RESOURCES OF NATURE.
...TO DEFEND OUR WOODS!

SPLOSH!
WORK STATION OUTPOST
WHEEE! I'M A WATER-PIG!

OR, WE COULD DO THAT.
RRGH! THWARTED BY MY OWN PIPEWORK!
SPLISH! SPLASH!

"THE WOBBLES!"

WHAT ON EARTH IS IT?
CAN I HUUUG IT?
IT SMELLS LIKE GRAVY!
I REALISED THERE WEREN'T ENOUGH ANIMALS IN THE WORLD, SO I DECIDED TO CREATE MY OWN!
I CALL IT THE WOBBLE.

IT LIVES ON A DIET OF CUSTARD, AND DOES LITTLE MORE THAN 'MEEP.'
MEEP!
BUT IT IS MINE. I MADE IT.
CUSTARD-O-MATIC

W...WHY IS IT SHAKING?
GOODNESS, I'M NOT SURE. TO BRING IT TO LIFE, I DID HAVE TO SET ITS PARTICLES TO A VERY HIGH VIBRATION.
MEEP! MEEP! MEEP! MEEP!

BANG!
SHRIEK!

AMAZING! IT IS...MULTIPLYING!
THEY ALL LOOK HUNGRY!
MEEP!
MEEP!
MEEP!

RELAX. I CREATED THIS, THE CUSTARD-O-MATIC, TO FEED THE FIRST WOBBLE. I'LL JUST SET IT TO A HIGHER SPEED!
MEEP!

WHAT IF...
CUSTARD-O-MATIC
MEEP!

WHAT IF THE WOBBLES KEEP MULTIPLYING?
THEN, UM...
THEN...
BANG!
BANG

MORE CUSTARD!
MORE CUSTARD!
SPLOOTCH!
SLOW DOWN, PIG!
BANG!
BANG!
THEY WON'T STOP APPEARING!
SIGHHH.
I'VE HAD EXPERIMENTS GO WRONG ENOUGH TIMES TO KNOW HOW THIS GOES NEXT.
FIVE MINUTES LATER...
A CUSTARD TIDAL WAVE! WELL DONE, SKUNKY!
THIS WASN'T MY FAULT!
NOT MY FAULT!
SPLOOOOOSH!

WELL, IT'S HEADING STRAIGHT FOR THE CITY! CAN YOU IMAGINE HOW MANY HUMANS WILL COME INTO OUR WOODS THEN?

PHEEEEP!!
DISCIPLINE IS WHAT THESE WOBBLES NEED.

PHEEP!
ALL OF YOU, LINE UP! I'VE NEVER SEEN SUCH AN UNRULY BUNCH OF GENETIC ABOMINATIONS.
MEEP!

WHATEVER YOU'RE DOING, LE FOX, I HOPE IT WORKS.
ME TOO.
SPLOOOSH!
CHOMP!

MEEP!
MEEP!
WELL, THE CITY'S SAFE, BUT WHAT DO WE DO WHEN SOMEONE DISCOVERS OUR WALL OF WOBBLES?
THE WOBBLES ATE ALL THE CUSTARD!
YAYY!
WE RUN AWAY!
EEK!
JAMIE

"BATTLE STATIONS!"

THE HUMANS ARE COMING!

THE HUMANS ARE COMING!

WE WERE PUTTING CUSTARD ON PIG'S HEAD, WHEN WE SAW ONE! HEADING THIS WAY!
SO. THEY'RE FINALLY INVADING.
WELL, WE ARE READY!

OPERATION DEFEND THE WOODS IS GO!
EVERYONE! TO YOUR DEFENCES!

PIG? WEENIE? WHY ARE YOU HIDING?
WE'RE GOING TO THROW PLASTIC SPOONS AT THEM!

THAT'S NOT REALLY... AUGH!
CREEEAK!
DID I RELEASE IT TOO SOON?

BE CAREFUL, MONKEY. MY DEFENCE IS A CHICKEN CANNON!

IT IS A VERY SENSITIVE DEVICE. ONE WRONG MOVE, AND...

...I'VE PRESSED THE WRONG BUTTON! EVERYONE RUN!
FRRPP!!
RUN!

CLUCK!!

WHAT ABOUT METAL STEVE? SURELY HE CAN HELP US?
OH, UMM... I FORGOT TO CHARGE HIM UP THIS MORNING.
SORRY.

THIS IS OUR BIG CHANCE TO DEFEND OURSELVES, AND IT'S ALL GONE WRONG!
IDIOTS.
I HAD THE BEST IDEA.

WE CAN HIDE, IN THE IMPENETRABLE PANIC ROOM, WHICH I BUILT BESIDE BUNNY'S HOUSE.
WHAT?

HOW COME I NEVER KNEW THIS WAS HERE?
YOU FORGET THINGS.
INSIDE, QUICKLY.
WE LOCK IT, AND NOW...
NOW WE SHH.

AHH! THE PEACE AND TRANQUILLITY OF NATURE!
SLAM!

THAT'S STRANGE. WHO WOULD BUILD A LITTLE HOUSE ALL THE WAY OUT HERE IN THE WOODS?

FART!
HEE HEE!
MMF!
SHH!
SHH-HH!

HUH.
AH WELL.

I THINK WE'RE SAFE. WHAT DO WE DO NOW, LE FOX?
WE WAIT...
WE WAIT A LONG TIME.

...OR UNTIL I REMEMBER HOW WE GET OUT OF HERE!
ARGH!

AUTUMN

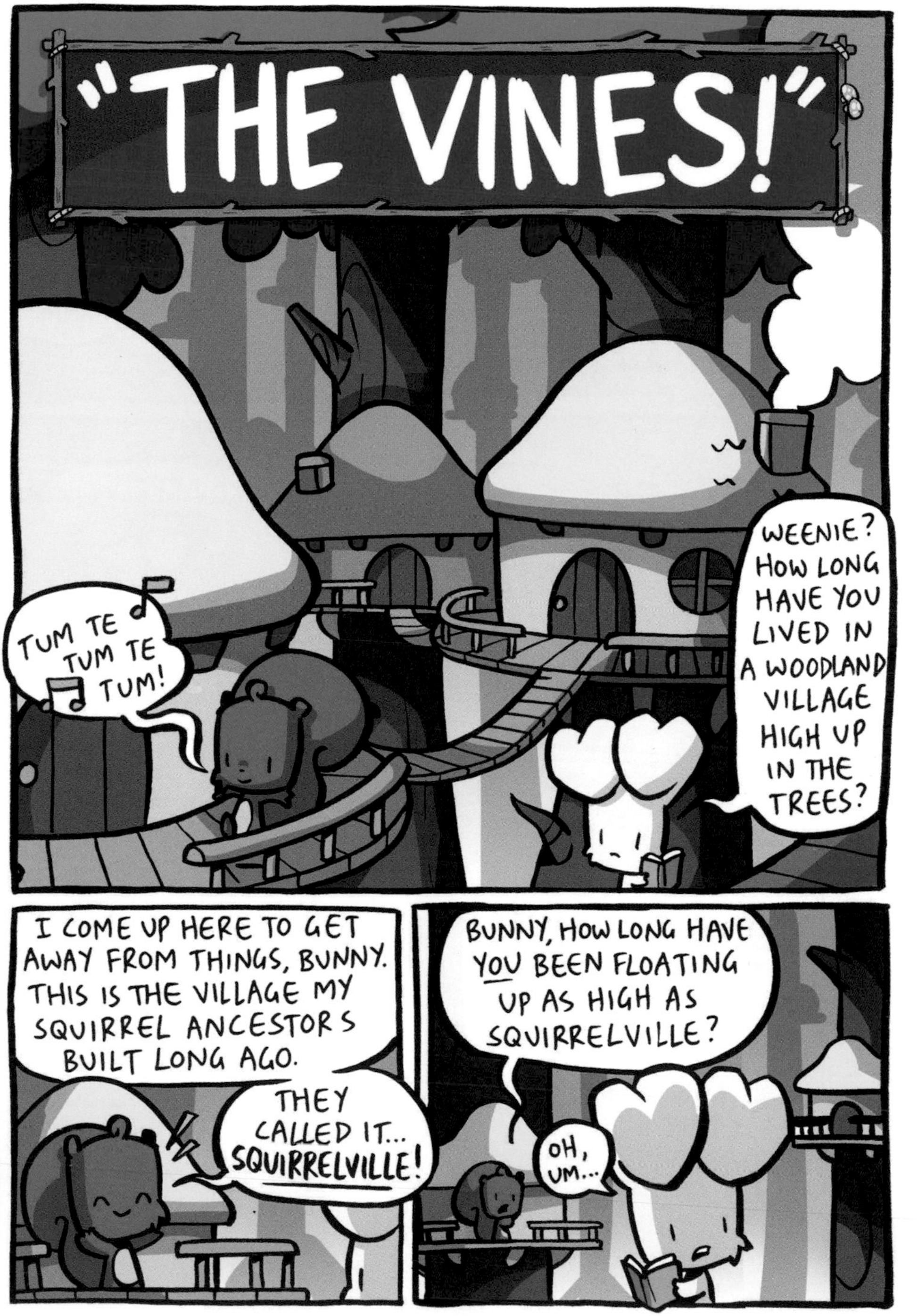

"THE VINES!"

TUM TE TUM TE TUM!

WEENIE? HOW LONG HAVE YOU LIVED IN A WOODLAND VILLAGE HIGH UP IN THE TREES?

AUGH!
I WASN'T PAYING ATTENTION, CLEARLY.
AUGH!

UH, BUNNY? YOU MIGHT WANT TO GET DOWN.
YOU'RE TELLING ME!
NO, SERIOUSLY. THE VINES ARE FAR MORE...
...UNSTABLE
...THAN I HAD PLANNED.

CRASH!
SQUIRRELVILLE!
SHRIEK!
AND HERRRE WE GO...
SIGH

THE DAY BEFORE...
SKUNKY, I DIDN'T WANT TO HAVE TO COME TO YOU, BUT NOW THE HUMANS ARE COMING INTO OUR WOODS, YOU'RE OUR BEST HOPE OF DEFENCE!
PLEASE, CREATE SOMETHING TO HELP US. TO SAVE THE WOODS. BUT DON'T GO MAD WITH SCIENCE, LIKE YOU USUALLY DO. TRY USING OUR SURROUNDINGS. USE NATURE.

YOU USED TOO MUCH SCIENCE!
NUH-UH!
I USED NATURE!

SKUNKY, WHAT HAVE YOU DONE?
OKAY, I USED A BIT OF SCIENCE.

SORRY.

MEANWHILE...
YOU STUPID MONKEY, WORK WITH US AGAINST THE HUMANS.
OR WE'LL ALL BE WITHOUT A HOME.

CRUMP!
OH WAIT, HERE'S ONE.

BOK!
ARGH!
EEK!

SCREAM!!
I'M BEING SICK EVERYWHERE!
I HOPE THIS WORKS.
BOOP!
GRAB!!
I CODED CONTROLS INTO THE VINES' DNA, TO PREVENT THEM RUNNING WILD!
JUST NEEDED TO CALIBRATE THE REMOTE CONTROL.
THE VINES!
THEY... SAVED US!
SCIENCE AND NATURE! I WIN! HERE, WEENIE, LET THE VINES REBUILD SQUIRRELVILLE.
YAY!
YAYYY!
SIGH
WAIT. IS NO ONE ELSE SCARED BY SKUNKY CONTROLLING NATURE?

"POINK!"

WHAT FOUL TERROR TORMENTS POOR PIG?

SHRIIIIII-IIIIIIIEK!

WHAT MALEFICENT FATE?

WHAT

THE HECK IS GOING ON?!

DON'T LET IT GET ME, BUNNY! I'M TOO PRETTY!
WHAT? WHAT'S GOING TO GET YOU?

OH.
WHERE'D HE GO?

POINK!
SHRIEK!
HA HAAA!
YOU'VE BEEN POINKED, BUNNY! NOW YOU ARE THE POINKER! AND UNLESS YOU CAN POINK SOMEONE ELSE...
...YOU'LL BE FOREVER POINKED!

SHRIIIIIIIEK!

I'M NOT PLAYING THIS...

...STUPID...
UM...

WAIT FOR ME!
GET AWAY, POINKER!

AHA! LOADS OF YOU TO POINK!
CAN'T POINK US.
ZIS IS POINK PRISON.

THEY WERE TOO ROUGH, BUNNY. TO POINK, ONE MUST DELICATELY POINK THE VICTIM.
ANY... "PUSHING, POKING, OR PARTICULARLY PERNICIOUS POINKING PRECIPITATES POINK PRISON".
RULES

SHRIEK! GET AWAY!

WHEN ARE WE ALLOWED OUT, ANYWAY?
I SAY WE BREAK OUT!
HRF!
EEE!

ALL PENALTIES ARE ABSOLVED! WE LIVE TO POINK AGAIN!
HEY! THAT'S CHEATING!
FLEE!

IT'S NOT CHEATING, LITTLE SQUIRREL, IF YOU NEVER LISTENED TO THE RULES IN THE FIRST PLACE.

POINK!
AHH NUTS!

POINK!
GET OFF ME.

POINK!
AARGH.

POINK!
NOOO!

POINK!
BIBBLE!

POINK!
BZZT!

POINK!
OW!

POINK, BUNNY!
WHAT? HOW'D IT END UP BACK AT ME?

SHRIIIEK!
WAIT...
BUT...
SHRIEK!
WHAT...
JAMIE

TWELVE HOURS LATER...
DO COME OUT, I'M SO TIRED.
MAN, BUNNY IS SO BAD AT THIS GAME.

"MONKEYTRON!"
SKUNKY, I'M STILL A LAUGHING STOCK IN THE WOODS. NO ONE FEARS ME!
I NEED YOUR HELP, BUT I'VE TRIED ALL YOUR INVENTIONS ALREADY.
SQUID-U-LIKE
WELL, NOT QUITE ALL.
THERE IS ONE THING I'VE BEEN HOLDING BACK.
JUST UNTIL YOU'RE READY TO USE IT.
SECRET!
THIS INVENTION WILL BE WHAT GRANTS YOU ULTIMATE POWER OVER THE REST OF US. IT IS TAILOR-MADE TO YOU, AND YOU ALONE.

BUT I'M ONLY TELLING YOU ABOUT IT TO SHOW OFF. THIS LEVEL OF AWESOME IS TOO DANGEROUS!
YOU CAN'T HAVE IT YET.

AW C'MON, I'LL GIVE YOU THIS CHEESE.
CHEESE! GO ON, THEN.

MEANWHILE, ABOVE GROUND...
IT IS IMPERATIVE WE TRAP THAT MONKEY AND BRING HIM BACK TO THE LAB.
TRAP!
MEH HEH!

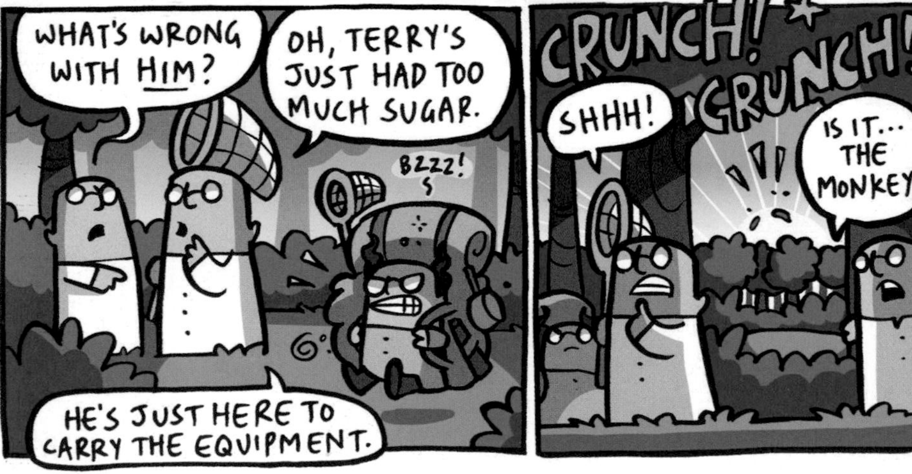
WHAT'S WRONG WITH HIM?
OH, TERRY'S JUST HAD TOO MUCH SUGAR.
BZZZ!
HE'S JUST HERE TO CARRY THE EQUIPMENT.
CRUNCH!
CRUNCH!
SHHH!
IS IT... THE MONKEY?

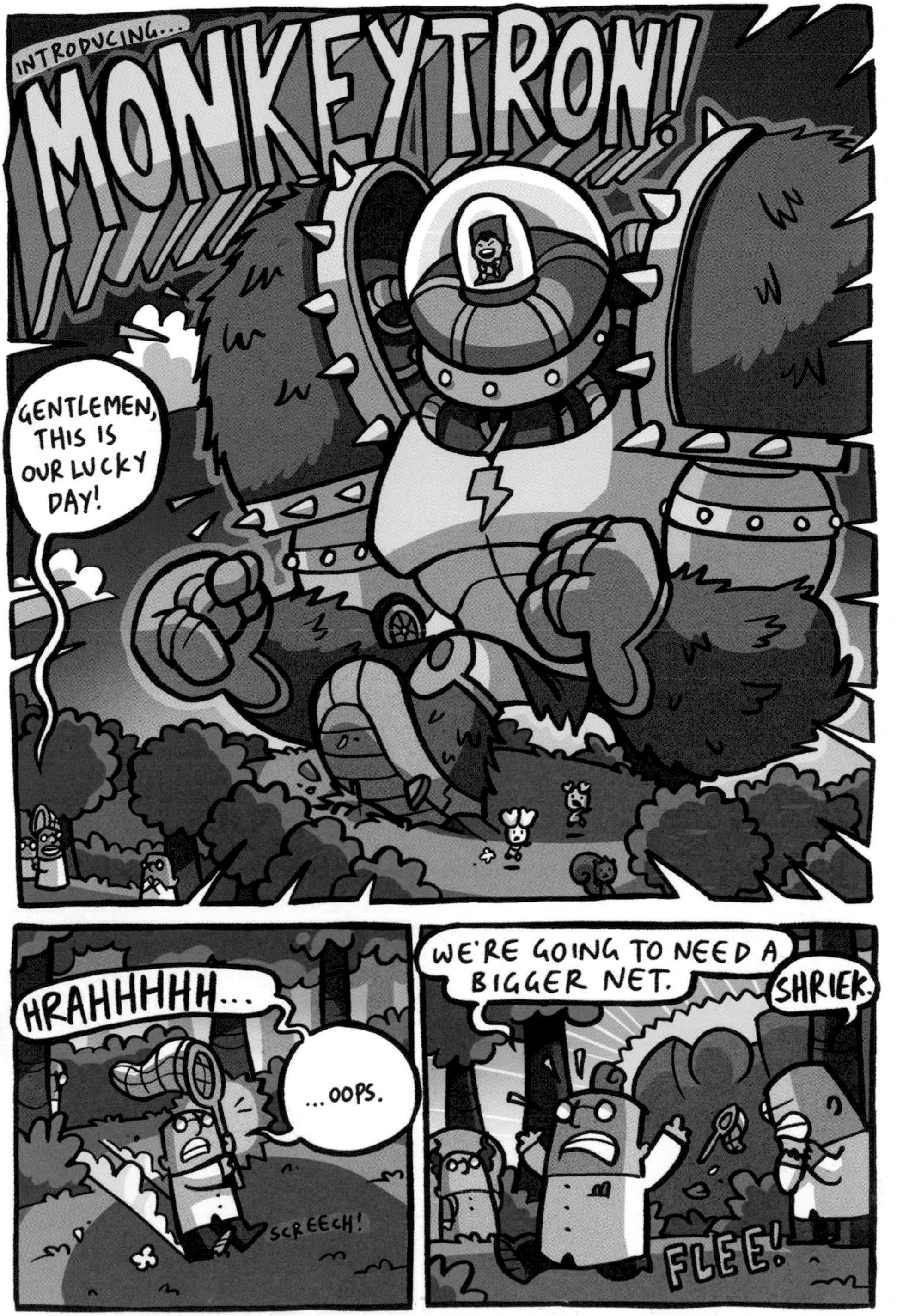

INTRODUCING...

MONKEYTRON!

GENTLEMEN, THIS IS OUR LUCKY DAY!

RUN, TERRY! WE DIDN'T BRING THE RIGHT EQUIPMENT FOR THAT!
OH, I DID.
A GOOD SCIENTIST COMES PREPARED FOR EVERY OUTCOME!
THIS MONKEY IS OURS!
IS THAT A BANANA?
IS THAT A BAZOOKA?
IT IS A BANANOOKA.
A BANAN...?
FSCHHH!
OOOKA!
TERRY! WHY DO YOU HAVE TO BLOW EVERYTHING UP?
MONKEY, WHY DO YOU HAVE TO BLOW EVERYTHING UP?
SKUNKY, WHY DOES EVERYTHING YOU CREATE BLOW UP?
AH, WHO CARES? I GOT CHEESE.

"A PIG ON THE RANGE"

TUESDAY, AND PIG IS READING HIS FAVOURITE WORK OF LITERATURE...

OINK OINK OINK GOES THE PIGGY.

MEH MEH MEH GOES THE LAMB!

BRUM BRUM BRUM GOES THE TRACTOR...
Tt IS FOR TRACTOR

...AND THEN HOME FOR EGGS AND HAM!
WHEE HEE HEEEE!
Tt
SKIP! SKIP!

AND THE REASON PIG LIKES THIS BOOK SO VERY MUCH...

...IS BECAUSE IT REMINDS HIM OF HOME.

GOOD MORNING, COUSIN GABE!
SNORT!
PIG?
MMF.

WELL HOWDY DOODY, COUSIN PIG! ABOUT TIME YOU CAME BACK, I'VE JUST BEEN RUSTLING UP SOME DELICIOUS TURNIPS FOR LUNCH!

WHAT IS IT YOU DO IN THOSE WOODS, ANYWAY?
UM. NOT MUCH.

PIG! SO NICE TO SEE OUR WANDERING SON AGAIN.
PIGGY WIGGY! YEEEE!

AND YOU'RE JUST IN TIME FOR A DELIGHTFUL SWILL LUNCH!
BUT... MY TURNIPS!

DON'T BE SILLY, GABE. THE HUMANS GIVE US ALL WE NEED!
SPTHBTHLOP!

SO...CHOMP...TELL US, YOUNG PIG. WHAT SIGHTS HAVE YOU SEEN? WHAT AMAZING ADVENTURES HAVE YOU HAD?
CHOMP!
CHOMP!
CHOMP!
UM...CHOMP... NOTHING?
CHOMP!

NONSENSE! YOU'RE THE WISEST AND BRAVEST OF ALL US PIGS. OF COURSE YOU HAVE STORIES TO TELL!

WELL, UM, THIS ONE TIME I DID A FART UNDERWATER.

AND IT ALL BUBBLED UP! HEE HEE HEE THPTHBTHH!
HEE!
SNORT!
HEE HEE!

CHOMP
CHOMP
CHOMP

AND SO, OFF PIG GOES AGAIN, LEAVING ONE FAMILY...

...FOR ANOTHER.
PIG! WHERE HAVE YOU BEEN?

UM, I CAN'T REMEMBER.
WELL, GET TOOLED UP! WE'RE DEFENDING OURSELVES AGAINST THE TERRIBLE HUMANS!
(HOWEVER CRAZY THEY MIGHT BE.)

"A BEAR BUM!"

I HAVE HAD IT WITH THESE WOODS. STRANGE NOISES, WEIRD EXPLOSIONS, SOMETHING IS GOING ON!

AND IF THE NATIONAL WOODLAND ASSOCIATION WON'T INVESTIGATE...
...THEN IT IS UP TO ME, PARK RANGER DEREK P. BRIGSTOCKE, TO UNCOVER THE TRUTH!

I JUST HOPE THE TRUTH IS NOTHING SCARY...
...OOPF!

GRRRWLL!
A...GRIZZLY BEAR IN...
A...
...NET?

SCREEEEEEEEEEAM!!
GRRRRRRWLLLLLLL!!

HMM.
THIS IS GOING TO BE A PROBLEM.

THAT NET WAS MEANT TO CATCH HUMANS, TO HELP US DEFEND THE WOODS. I WASN'T EXPECTING THE BEAR TO GET CAUGHT IN IT!
HEE HEE. SILLY BEAR.

THE QUESTION IS, HOW DO WE GET THE BEAR DOWN, WITHOUT THE HUMAN SEEING US?
BLOO BLOO BLOO!

RO-PIG HOOD WILL FIX THIS!
BLOO BLOO!
PTOO!

SNAP!

CRUMP!
ARGH! NO!
THIS IS WORSE!

OOPS.
PIG, NEXT TIME YOU HAVE AN IDEA, CHECK WITH US FIRST.
STAND ASIDE, CHUMPS!

LUCKY FOR US ALL, I HAPPEN TO HAVE INVENTED A...
...BEAR VACUUM!
IT'S SHAPED LIKE A TANK. I LIKE TANKS.

VMMMMMMMMMMMMMN!
IT'S WORKING! IT'S W...

THUNK!
...IT'S STUCK!
MY GENIUS PLAN, THWARTED BY A BEAR BUM!
HEE HEE.
HEE HEE.
HEE HEE.
BEAR BUM.
HEE HEE.
GRRF.
A BARE BUM.
HEE HEE.
HEH.
HEE.
FAINT!
URGHH.
NOW'S OUR CHANCE!
WE'LL LEAVE HIM THERE TILL HE WAKES UP. THANKS AGAIN FOR YOUR HELP, BEAR!
GRRF.*
*-S'ALRIGHT.

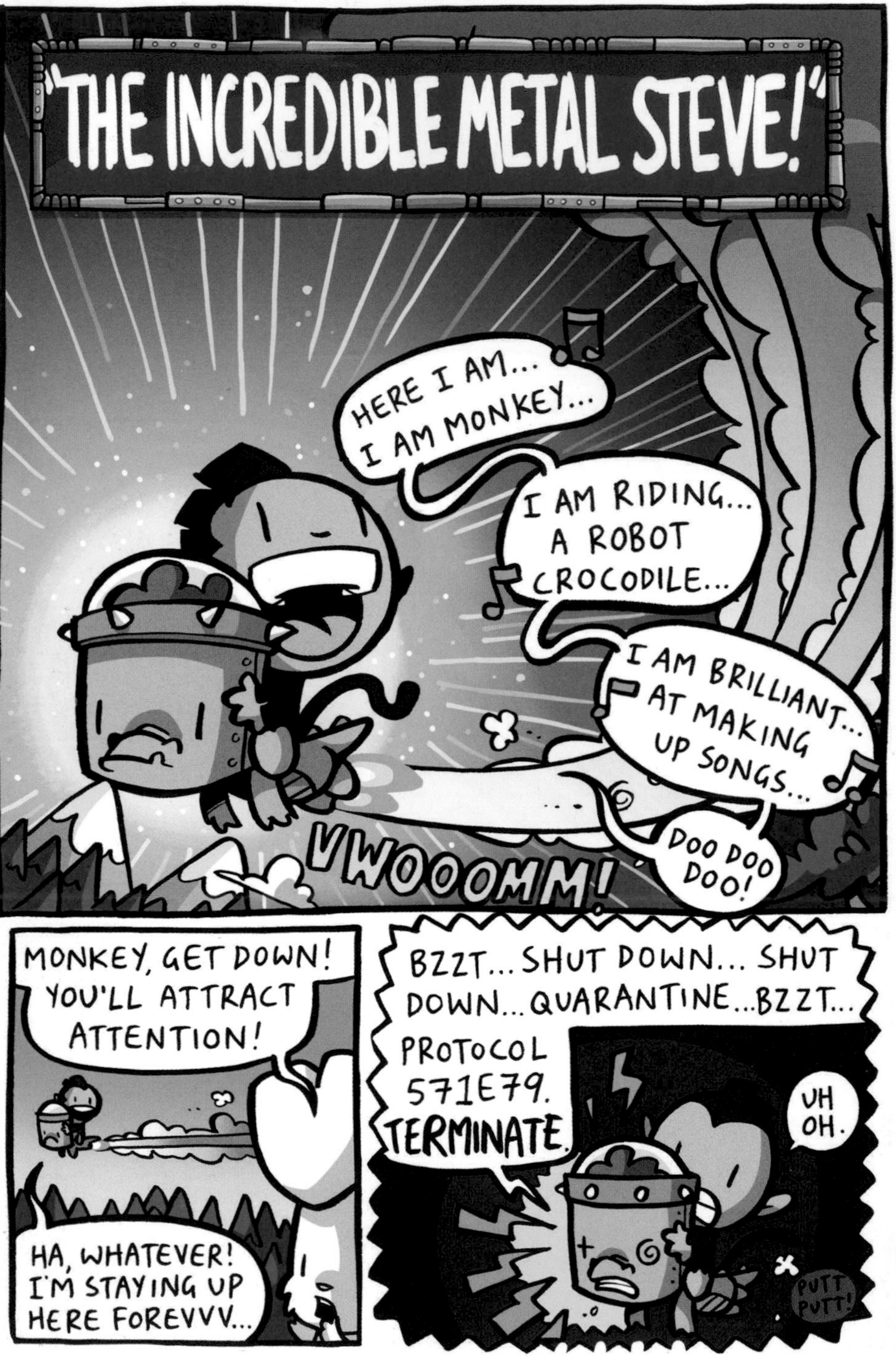

"THE INCREDIBLE METAL STEVE!"

HERE I AM... I AM MONKEY...
I AM RIDING... A ROBOT CROCODILE...
I AM BRILLIANT... AT MAKING UP SONGS...
DOO DOO DOO!
VWOOOOMM!

BEEEYOOOOOOO!
SCREEEEEEAMM!
SIGHHH.

STUPID ROBOT CROCODILE! I WAS SO SCARED I NEARLY DID AN EMERGENCY WEE!

IT IS HAPPENING AGAIN.

ZAT 'ROBOT' PICKS UP RADIO SIGNALS WHEN HE FLIES OVER CERTAIN PARTS OF THE WOODS. THEY INTERFERE WITH HIS BRAIN.
I SUSPECT ZE REASON WHY IS TO BE FOUND...

...IF WE LOOK DOWN!
GAAASP!

WHAT... WHAT IS IT?
SOME KIND OF METAL PLAQUE, STUCK IN THE GROUND, TRANSMITTING A SIGNAL!
I HAVE SEEN OTHERS LIKE IT AROUND ZE WOODS.

YEAH WELL, IF THIS THING BROUGHT STEVE DOWN...
MAYBE IT CAN CHARGE HIM BACK UP!

....

BWOOM
VTTT!
SKK!
KRR!
ALPHA MODE... INITIATED.

...BEGIN COUNTDOWN TO CATASTROPHIC DESTRUCTION IN...
3...
2...

HE'S...HE'S BECOME A MONSTER!

A MONSTER?
BZZT!
WHERE?

VVT! ZZT! KRR! SKK!
BZZT! RETREAT! RETREAT!

SCREEEAMM!
BZZT! WAIT FOR ME!

WILL YOU LOT STOP JUMPING AROUND ON MY ROOF?!
JAMIE

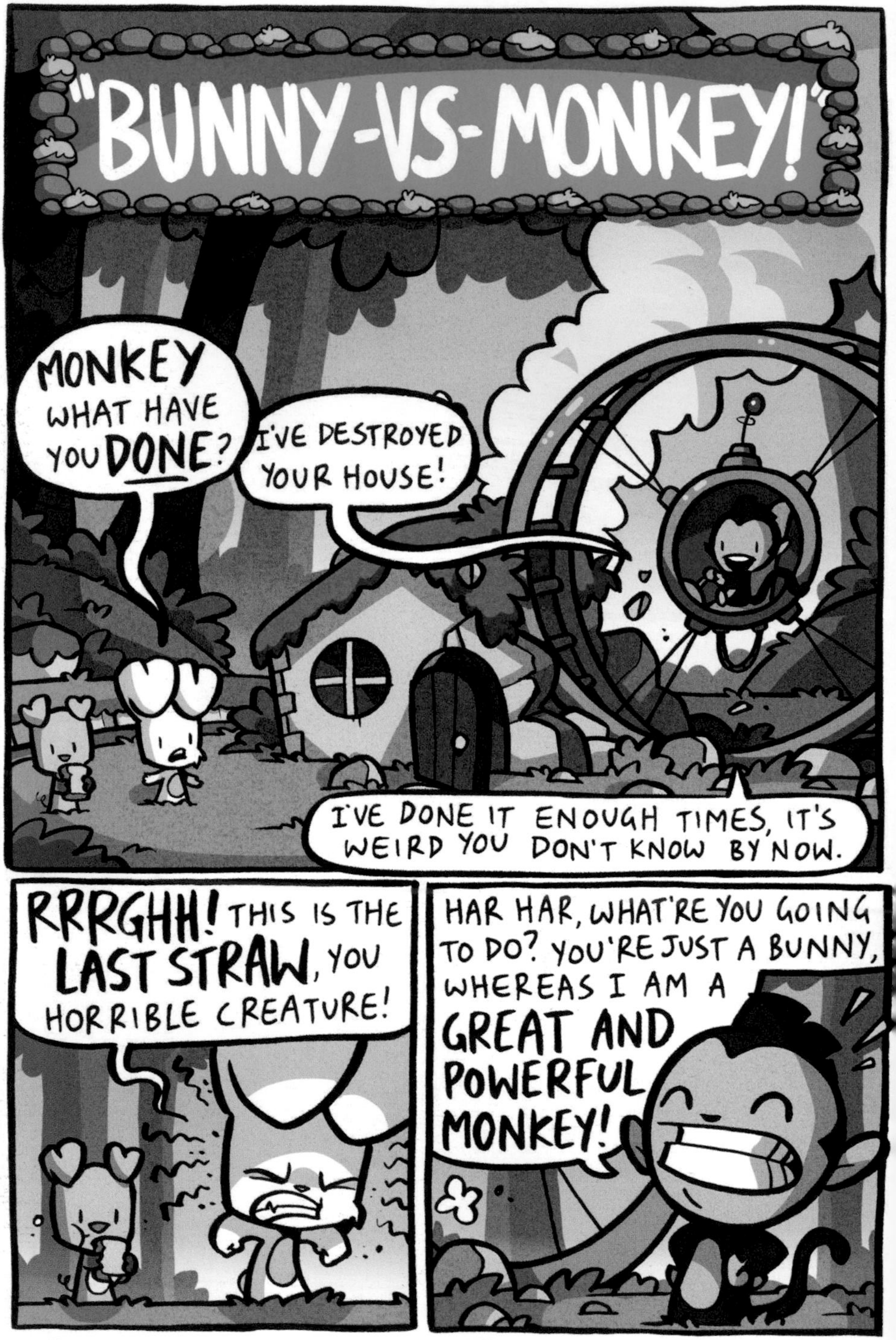

"BUNNY-VS-MONKEY!"

MONKEY WHAT HAVE YOU DONE?

I'VE DESTROYED YOUR HOUSE!

I'VE DONE IT ENOUGH TIMES, IT'S WEIRD YOU DON'T KNOW BY NOW.

BLAT!!
EUGH.

DID YOU JUST THROW MY SANDWICH?
COME AT ME, MONKEY! LET'S SORT THIS OUT ONCE AND FOR ALL!

GAH! IF HE'S ALLOWED TO USE WEAPONS, THEN SO AM I! SKUNKY, WHAT WEAPONS DO YOU HAVE ON YOU?
UMM...

ONLY THIS HIGHLY VOLATILE TICKING BOMB! BUT IF IT BLEW UP, YOU'D BE CAUGHT IN THE BLAST TOO!
00:00
TICK!
TICK!

A BOMB? HA! WHAT ARE YOU GOING TO DO, HIT ME WITH IT?
TICK!
TICK!

CLONK!
YES.
OW!

SERIOUSLY, MONKEY. YOU SHOULDN'T... OW!!
QUIET, SCIENCE!
CLONK!

NO ONE WILL DEFEAT ME! I AM EMPEROR MONK...
LUZZ!

OOF!!
MY PUDDING!
LUZZ!

HRR-RAR-RGHHLE!
BLARR-RGLEF!

CLONK! SPLAT! CLONK! OOF! CLONK! FRRP! CLONK! ARGH!

SOME TIME LATER...
PHEW! I'M EXHAUSTED! WE CAN'T KEEP FIGHTING FOREVER.
AGREED.

A TRUCE, THEN. AN ARMISTICE. WE AGREE TO RESPECT EACH OTHER'S BOUNDARIES.

CLONK!
NO. LET ME WIN.

BOOM!
I DID WARN HIM.

YOU'RE SO STUPID, MONKEY! WHY CAN'T YOU DO ANYTHING RIGHT?
YOU SHUTTING UP WOULD BE NICE. I'LL DO THAT.
CLONK!
SIGHH..
JAMIE

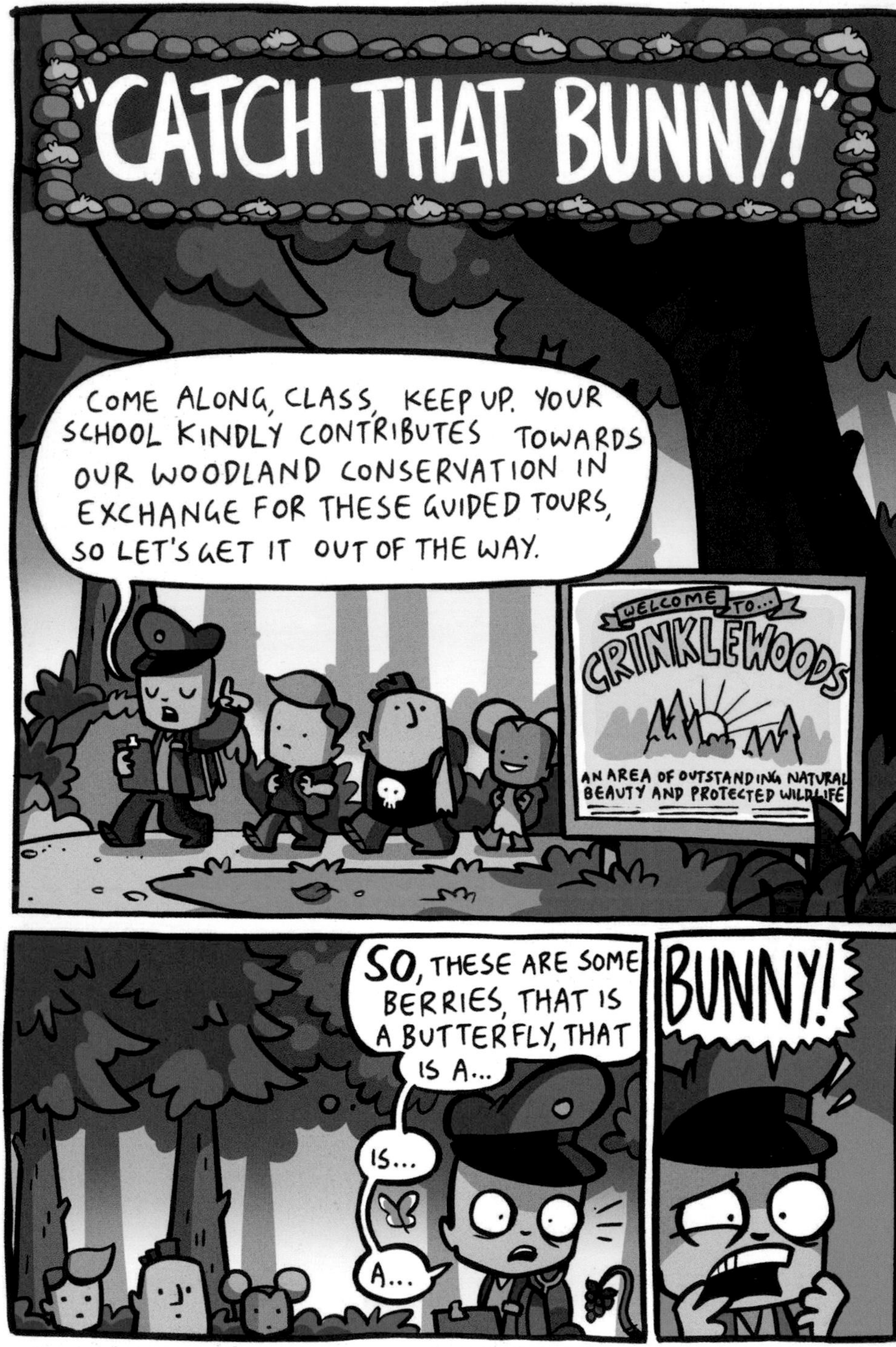

"CATCH THAT BUNNY!"

COME ALONG, CLASS, KEEP UP. YOUR SCHOOL KINDLY CONTRIBUTES TOWARDS OUR WOODLAND CONSERVATION IN EXCHANGE FOR THESE GUIDED TOURS, SO LET'S GET IT OUT OF THE WAY.

WELCOME TO...
CRINKLEWOODS
AN AREA OF OUTSTANDING NATURAL BEAUTY AND PROTECTED WILDLIFE

WEIRD THINGS HAPPEN IN THESE WOODS. WEIRD, EXPLODEY, THINGS. AND THAT BUNNY ALWAYS SEEMS TO BE IN THE MIDDLE OF IT.

AS IF HE'S IN CHARGE OR SOMETHING.

BECAUSE WE MUST
CATCH THAT BUNNY!
HE'S RUNNING!
SO MUCH FOR STEALTH, THEN!
HOP!
GRAB HIM!!
HE'LL BE DELICIOUS!
RUN, BUNNY!
THERE HE IS!
WE GOT HIM CORNERED!
HAR HAR! YOU FELL RIGHT INTO OUR TRAP!
WHAT?

LOOK INTO THE EYES OF THE HYPNO-MONKEY, FOOLISH MORTALS! SLIP INTO MY HYPNOTIC GAAAAAZE.
MESMERISE!

NOW, TELL US EVERYTHING YOU KNOW ABOUT THE ROAD BEING BUILT. GIVE US ALL YOUR HUMAN KNOWLEDGE!

BUHHHHHH...

OH, AND ONE MORE THING...

I DON'T LIKE WORKING WITH YOU, SKUNKY. ESPECIALLY NOT AS BAIT.
YOU WERE RUBBISH BAIT. THEY KNEW NOTHING.
WILL THEY BE OKAY?

OH, THEY'LL BE FINE.
TOMORROW.
BUCK-CAW!
CLUCK CLUCK!
DOODLE DOOO!
CLUCK! CLUCK!
PECK! PECK!
JAMIE

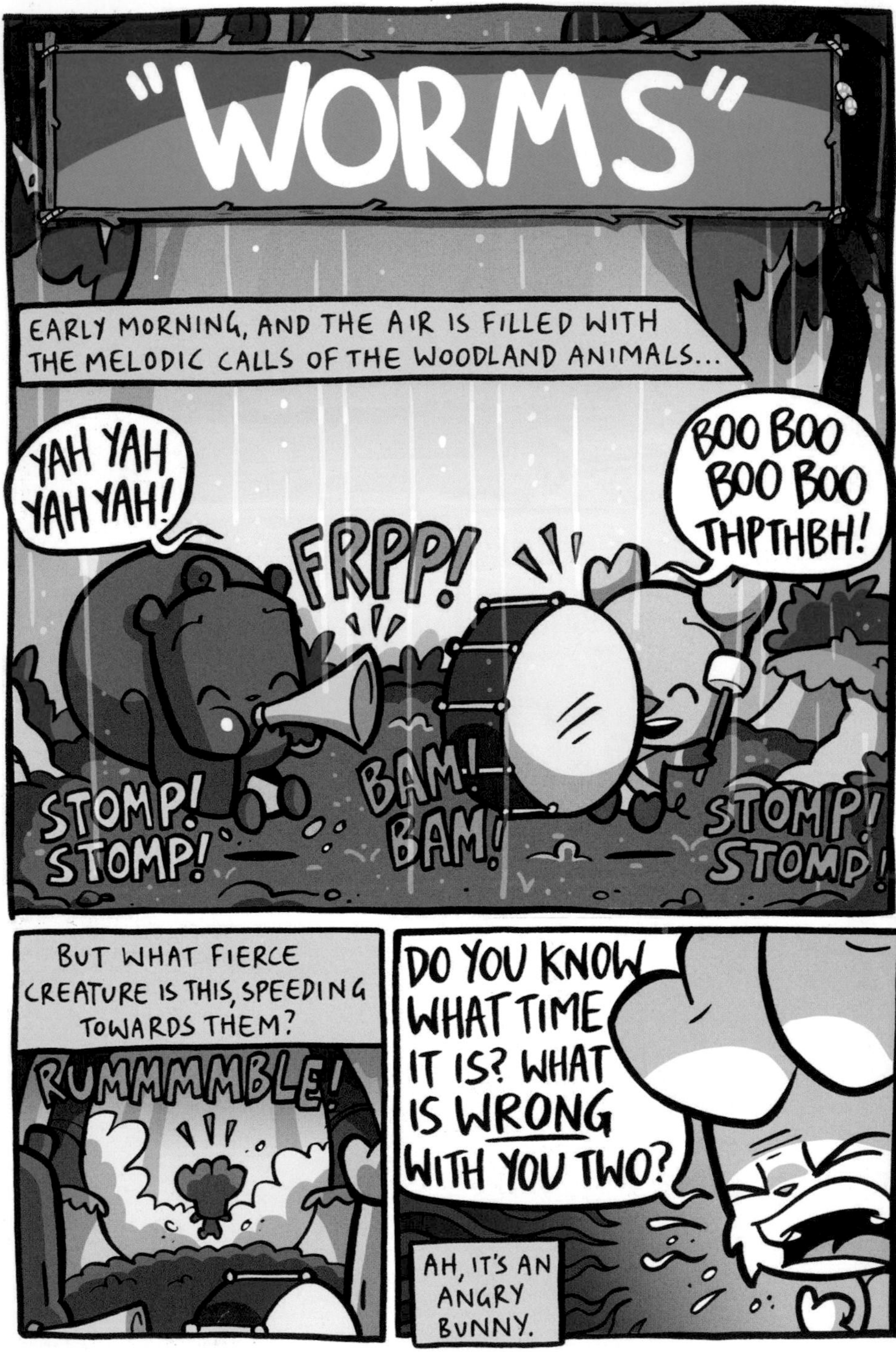

"WORMS"

EARLY MORNING, AND THE AIR IS FILLED WITH THE MELODIC CALLS OF THE WOODLAND ANIMALS...

YAH YAH YAH YAH!

FRPP!

BOO BOO BOO BOO THPTHBH!

STOMP! STOMP!

BAM! BAM!

STOMP! STOMP!

DID WE WAKE YOU, BUNNY?
SOMEHOW, YES.

WE'RE TRYING TO WAKE UP THE WORMS! WHILE IT'S RAINING AND EARLY IN THE MORNING IS THE BEST TIME!
THE...WHAT?

THE WORMS! IF YOU MAKE A LOT OF NOISE, THEY COME OUT OF THE GROUND!
STOMP! STOMP!

I'VE NEVER HEARD ANYTHING SO RIDICU...
POP!
EEE!!

IT WORKED! IT WORKED!
THEY'VE ALL COME UP TO SEE WHAT'S GOING ON!
POP!
POP!
POP!
POP!

WHAT EXACTLY ARE YOU GOING TO DO WITH ALL THESE WORMS?

A WORM HAT!

A WORM PIE!
UGH!

ONLY JOKING. WE'RE GOING TO TAKE THEM DOWN TO THE RIVER AND DO SOME FISHING!

FISHING? THEY'RE BAIT? AFTER ALL THAT, YOU'RE GOING TO LET THE WORMS GET EATEN BY FISH?
CLONK!
CLONK!

NO, SILLY. EUGH! WE BROUGHT THE WORMS DOWN TO WATCH US FISH!
WE THOUGHT THEY MIGHT ENJOY IT.

BUT THEN, HOW ARE YOU GOING TO GET THE FISH OUT OF THE WATER?
WELL, DUHHH...

YAH YAH YAH YAH!
BOO BOO BOO BOO THPTBTH!
FRPP!
BANG!
BANG!
BANG!
HOW SILLY OF ME.

"GOOD BYE BUNNY"
ONE COLD WINTER'S MORNING, BUNNY WAS STANDING INSIDE HIS HOUSE, STARING OUT OF THE WINDOW...
HE WAS LOOKING AT THE WOODS HE LOVED SO MUCH...
THE ONLY WOODS HE KNEW...
HE WATCHED HIS WOODLAND FRIENDS PLAYING ON THE GRASS...

I AM SIR CHUFFINGTON, THE KNIGHT!
AND I AM LORD WUFFYWUFF, THE LUNCHTIME!
HAVE AT YE!
CRUMP!!
OWWW!
BOO HOO!
BOO HOO HOO!

AND JUST THEN, SOMETHING OCCURRED TO BUNNY THAT HE'D NEVER BEEN ABLE TO PUT INTO WORDS BEFORE...
I DON'T BELONG HERE.

NO, YOU DON'T.
SHRIEK! LE FOX! HOW DID YOU GET IN?
I DUG A TUNNEL UNDER YOUR FLOOR. SO WHAT? CARRY ON.

I'VE FELT THIS WAY FOR A WHILE, LE FOX. I CAN'T EXPLAIN IT, I JUST KNOW THIS ISN'T MY HOME.
WHERE IS YOUR HOME THEN?

I DON'T KNOW. BUT FOR AS LONG AS I CAN REMEMBER, I'VE HAD THIS BOX.
AND INSIDE THIS BOX LIES THE ANSWER!

I HAVE TO GO. I'LL PACK A FEW THINGS, AND GO OUT INTO THE WORLD.
TO DISCOVER WHERE I CAME FROM, AND FIND OUT WHO I AM.
ISN'T THAT THE MOST IMPORTANT THING?

WHY DO I HAVE SO MANY CARROTS?
I DON'T EVEN LIKE CARROTS!

GOODBYE, EVERYONE! I HAVE TRIED TO FIT IN, BUT I CAN'T STAY HERE ANY LONGER!
BUNNY, NO! WE MADE YOU A CAKE!

WELL, WE MADE A CAKE. LAST WEEK.
THERE ARE STILL SOME CRUMBS OF IT IN MY BELLY, IF YOU WANT THEM.

BUNNY? GOING? AT LAST, I CAN TAKE OVER THE WOODS!
YOU WON'T, MONKEY. IT'LL GO WRONG, LIKE ALWAYS.
BAH! I SUPPOSE!

HE'S LEAVING?
WHAT DID HE FIND OUT?
CLANK! CLANK!
NOTHING. BUT THERE IS A BOX.
WHAT'S IN THE BOX?

PLEASE CONTACT: 15, BRAMBLE CRESCENT MIDDLETON, THE CITY

YOU WILL ALL BE FINE WITHOUT ME.
YOU MUST HAVE BEEN BEFORE.

BUT...BUT WHO'LL HELP ME CLIMB BACK OUT WHEN I FALL IN A HOLE?
I THINK YOU'RE GOING TO HAVE TO START DOING THAT FOR YOURSELF, PIG.
JAMIE

WINTER

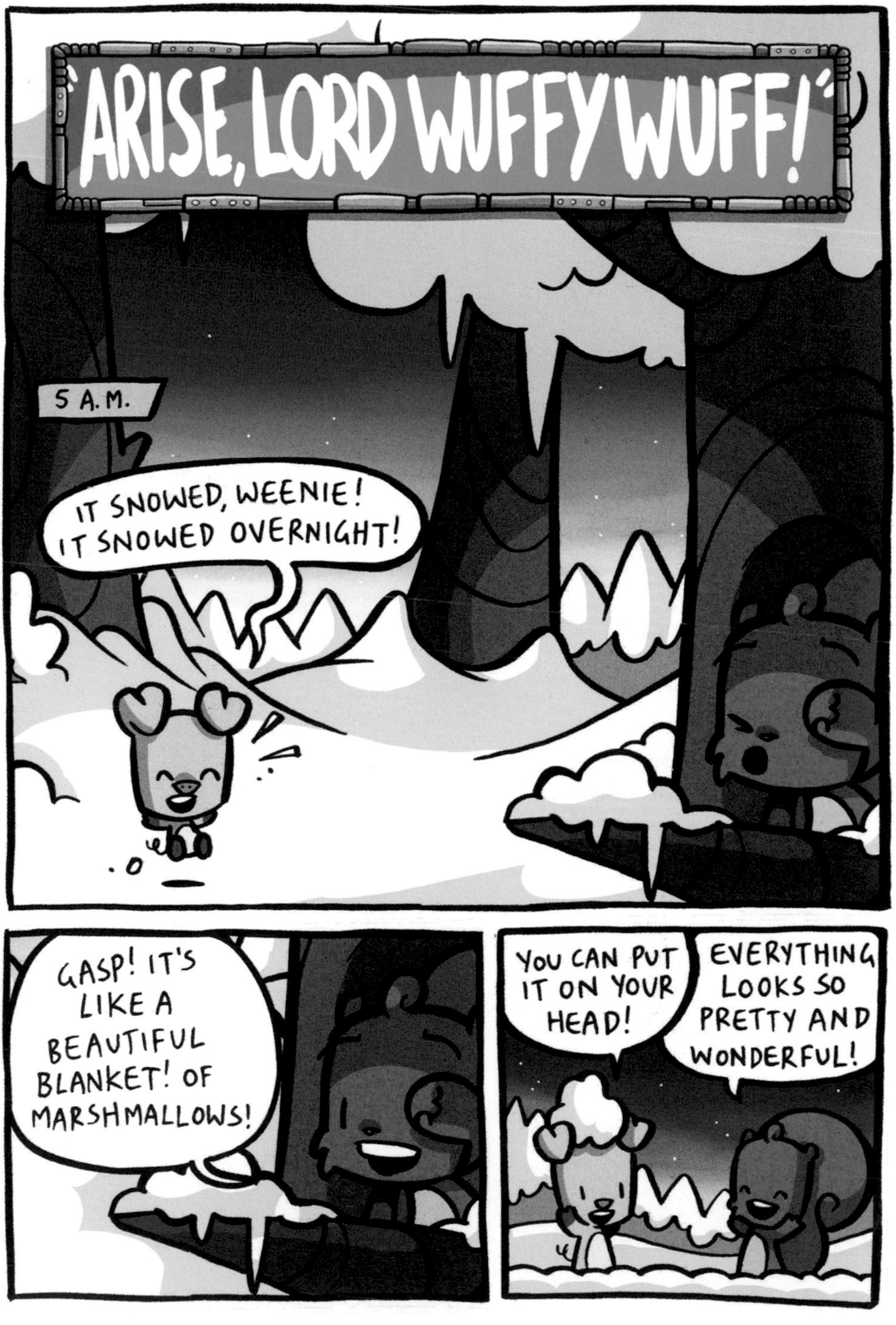

ARISE, LORD WUFFYWUFF!

5 A.M.

IT SNOWED, WEENIE! IT SNOWED OVERNIGHT!

EUGH! IT'S DISGUSTING!
FWOOM!

MORNING, IDIOTS! DON'T WORRY, WE'LL HAVE THIS SNOW MELTED AWAY IN MINUTES!

WITH BUNNY GONE, I'M FREE TO TAKE OVER THE WOODS!
AND I'LL DO IT BY SCORCHING THE EARTH, RIDING ON SKUNKY'S LATEST INVENTION... THE BLACK DRAGON!
FWOOM!
WE NEED HELP!
!
I KNOW JUST WHO!

LORD WUFFYWUFF, THE KNIGHT!
WE'RE SAVED! SAVED!

HALT, FOUL DRAGON! FOR I AM A KNIGHT, AND I SLAY...
HEE HEE SHHH!
HEE HEE!
I SLAY DRAGONS FOR BREAKFAST!

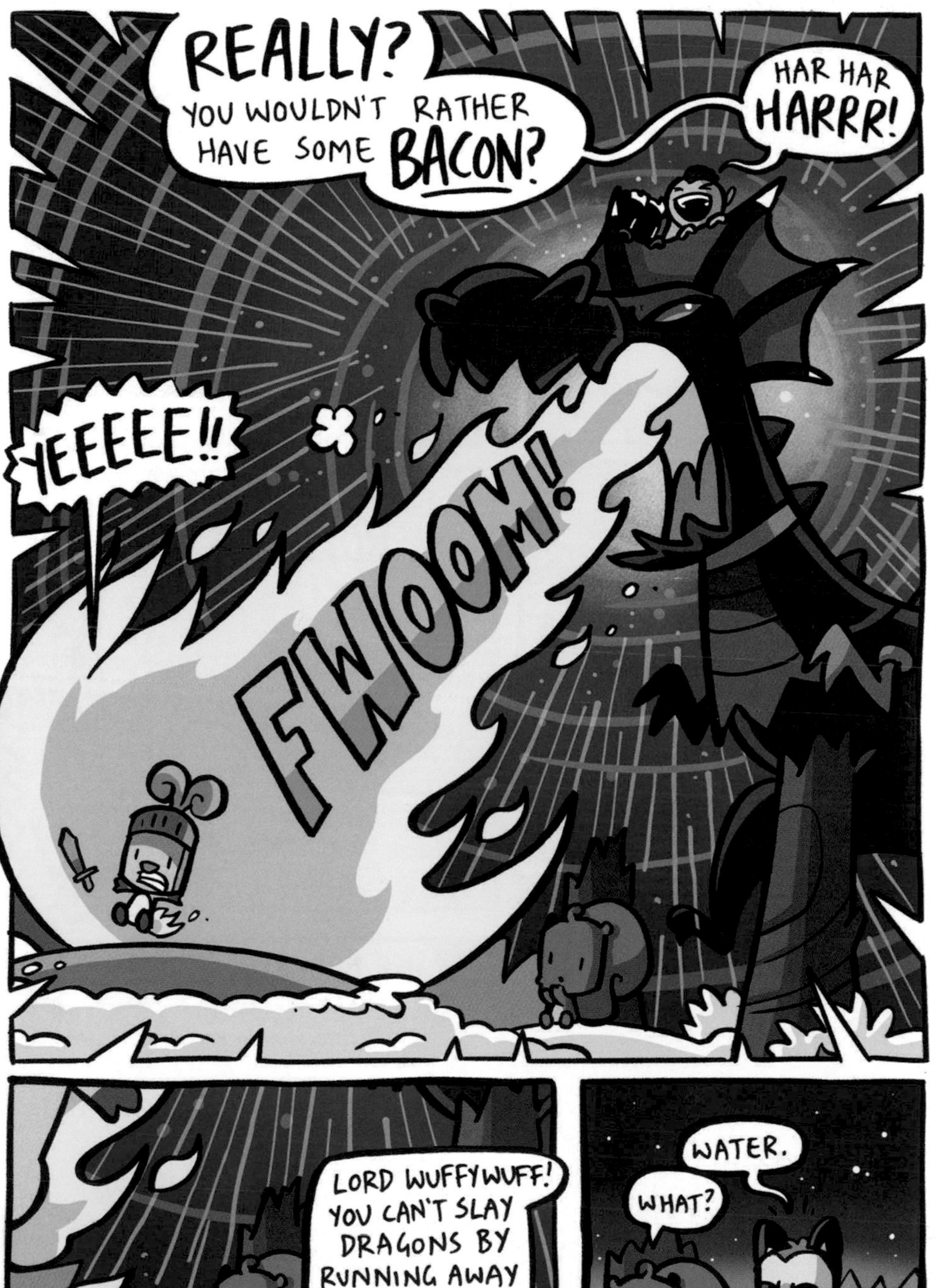

REALLY? YOU WOULDN'T RATHER HAVE SOME BACON?
HAR HAR HARRR!
YEEEEE!!
FWOOM!

POUR WATER ONTO WHERE THE DRAGON HAS CLEARED THE SNOW.
WHY?
IT'LL FREEZE. IT BECOMES...
SPLOSH!

...ICE!
SLIP!
SLIP!
ARGH! STOPPIT!

WHEEEEE! THIS WAY, DRAGONNY-PLOPS!
FREEZE!
SLIP!
I CAN'T CONTROL IT! EEEE!!

NOT THE LAKE! NOT THE LAKE!
CRASH!!

BZZT!
FZZT!
HEE HEE! NOW IT'S A DRA-GONE!
I CAN TAKE THE DEFEAT, JUST SPARE ME THE PUNS.

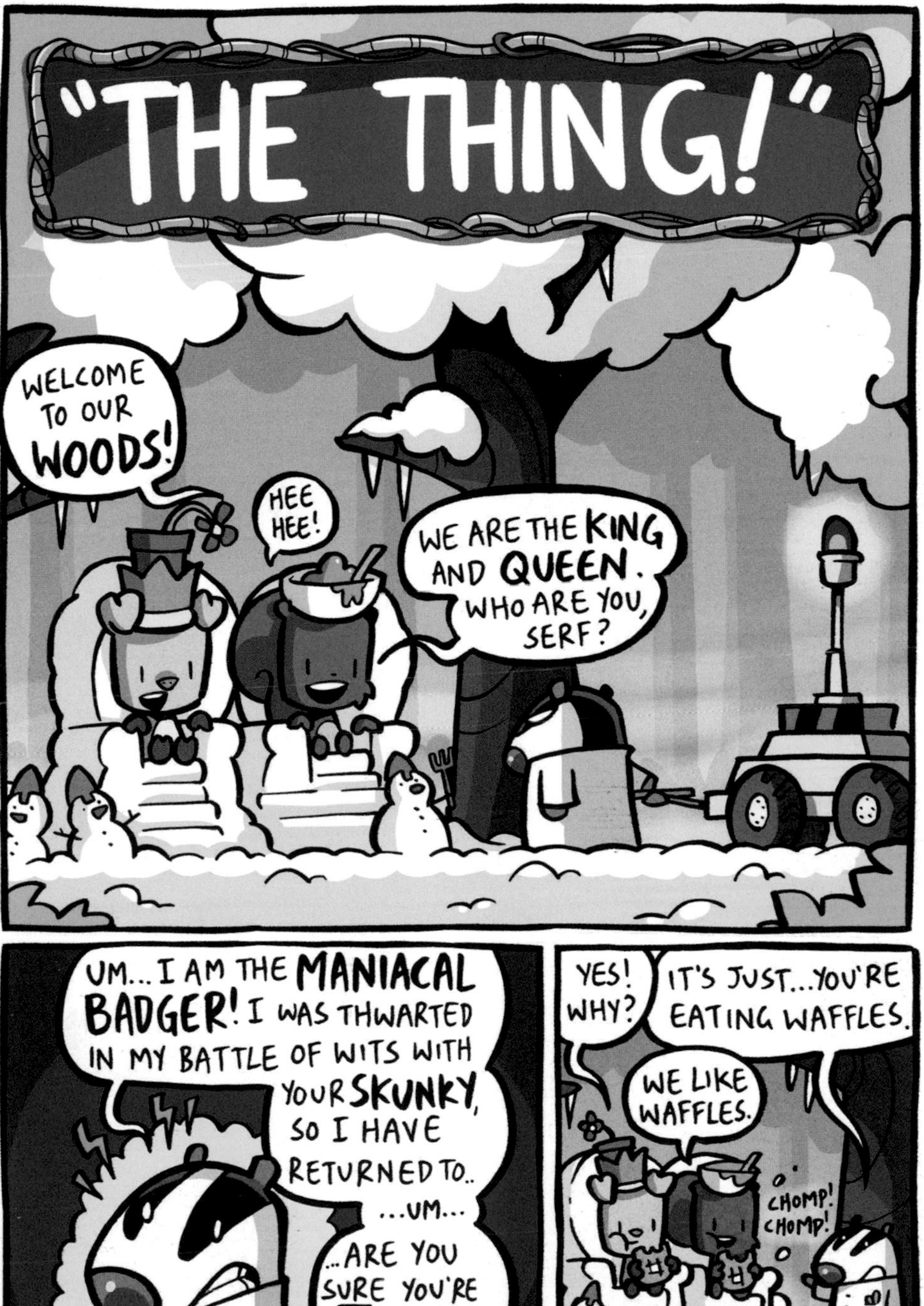

"THE THING!"

WELCOME TO OUR WOODS!
HEE HEE!
WE ARE THE KING AND QUEEN. WHO ARE YOU, SERF?

SINCE BUNNY LEFT THE WOODS, THERE HAS BEEN A LACK OF ORDER AND CONTROL. SO WE MADE OURSELVES ROYALTY!
WE'RE IN CHARGE!
GIGGLE!

WELL, CAN I GET PAST?
NOT UNTIL YOU'VE WATCHED KING PIG DO SPINS ON HIS HEAD!
HEE HEE! I CAN DO IT!

SIGH...
I CAN'T DO IT!
YOU CAN, PIG! I BELIEVE IN YOU!

YOU!
YEWWWW!
COME BACK FOR MORE, EH?
NO! I MEAN, YES!
I MEAN, I'LL WIN THIS TIME.
OH, YOU WILL?
I WON'T!
I MEAN, YES! I WILL!

YOU FOOL, I AM SKUNKY! GENIUS OF THE WOODS!
MASTER OF DEVIOUS INVENTION!
NONE CAN DEFEAT MY BRILLIANT BRAIN!

AH, BUT YOU DON'T HAVE ONE...
OF THESE!
WHAT... WHAT IS THAT?
IT IS... A THING.

HEY! IS IT SOMETHING THAT COULD DESTROY US ALL? I BET IT IS!
HOW BRILLIANT.
DO NOT MOVE!

LET ME HAVE A GO ON IT!
GERROFF! IT'S NOT YOURS! YOU'LL BREAK IT!
DO NOT MOVE!

DON'T YOU KNOW WHO I AM? I AM MONKEY, FUTURE EMPEROR OF THIS DISGUSTINGLY BEAUTIFUL PLANET!
ANY CATASTROPHIC WEAPONS ARE MINE!

ALL OF YOU, GET AWAY. IT IS NOT TO BE PLAYED WITH!
THANK YOU.

IT IS MINE! I AM LE FOX, GUARDIAN OF THESE WOODS.
AND I AM CONFISCATING THIS THING IN ZE INTERESTS OF ALL OUR SAFETY.
AND SO I CAN HAVE A PLAY WITH IT.

AH, HERE IT IS.
BIFF!
SCRAP!
OW!
FOUND IT, BERT.

ALIGNMENT BEACON 15B, FOR HELPING US PLOT WHERE TO BUILD THE MOTORWAY.
?
MAP
BUT WHO DRAGGED IT OUT HERE?

WHO CARES? IF THE THING'S HERE, THEN HERE IS WHERE WE BUILD THE ROAD.
RIGHTY-HO.

WEENIE?
PIG?

ABDICATE! ABDICATE! WE NEED BUNNY BACK!
BUNNYYY!

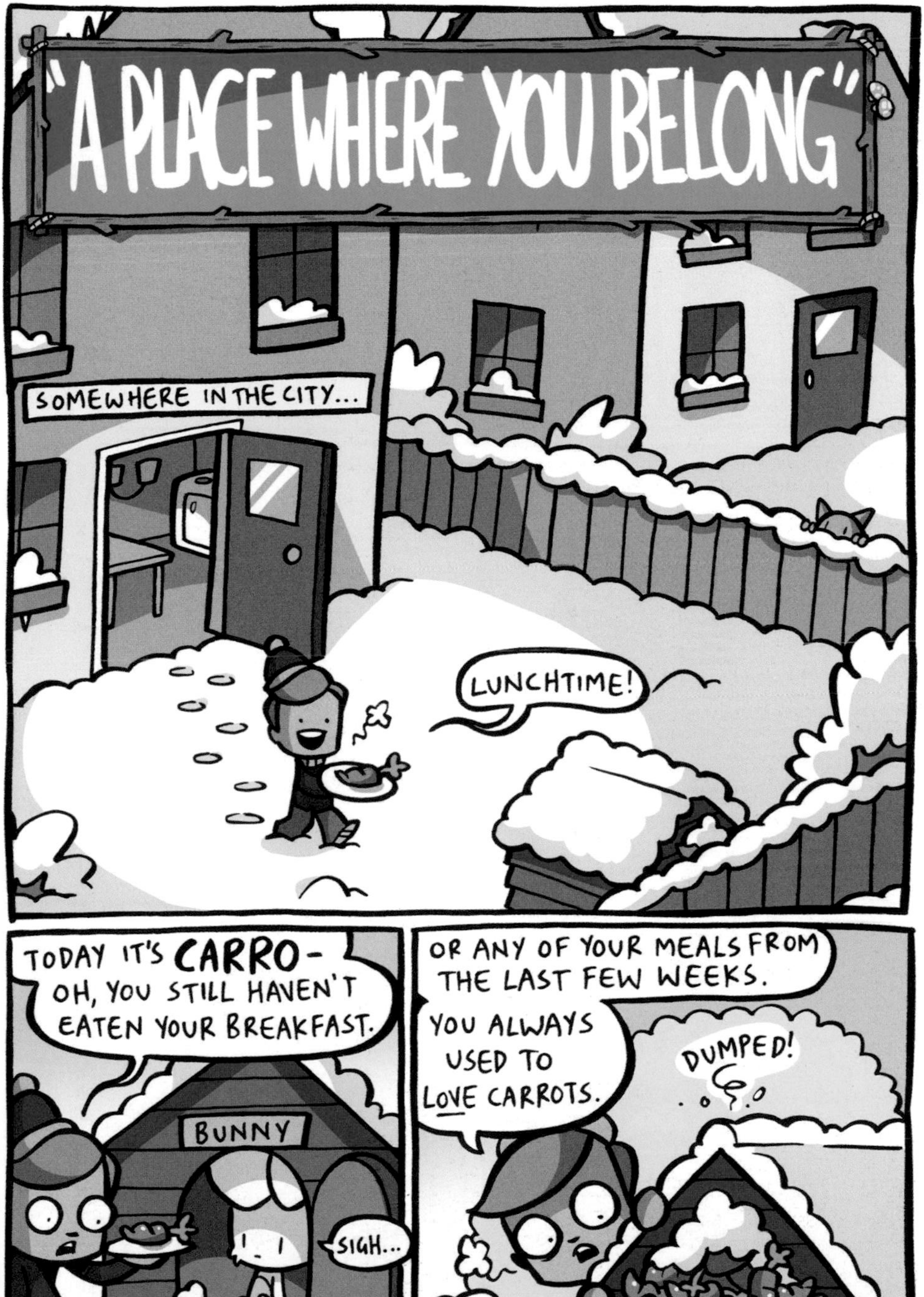

"A PLACE WHERE YOU BELONG"

SOMEWHERE IN THE CITY...

LUNCHTIME!

I'M SO GLAD YOU'RE BACK, BUNNY. I PUT THESE POSTERS UP ALL OVER TOWN, BUT WHEN I SAW YOU IN THE WOODS...

LOST
BUNNY
IF SEEN
PLEASE CONTACT
...WELL, I KNEW YOU'D COME HOME.

I'LL GO AND GET YOU SOMETHING NICE TO EAT, YOU MUST BE STARVING BY NOW.
BUNNY

NAH, I BROUGHT SANDWICHES AND CHOCOLATE WITH ME...
HOME SWEET HOME
PSST! HEY, BUNNY!

I'VE COME TO BUST YOU OUT!
RANDOLPH!

AND I BROUGHT SOME FRIENDS!
WEENIE! PIG!

BUST ME OUT? BUT MY NEW HOUSE HAS A FRONT DOOR, I CAN JUST WALK OUT.
THEN... WHY ARE YOU STILL HERE?

THIS IS WHERE I BELONG! THE FOOD'S NOT GREAT, BUT I'M SAFE AND LOOKED AFTER, AND I HAVE A WHOLE GARDEN TO RUN AROUND IN!
I'M BACK HOME. I CAN'T EVEN REMEMBER WHY I LEFT!

SOUNDS WELL BORING. I FOUND THESE TWO WANDERING AROUND THE CITY, COVERED IN ICE CREAM.
WE FELL IN AN ICE CREAM, BUNNY!
OVER AND OVER AGAIN!

I DON'T THINK THEY'RE HANDLING BEING IN THE CITY VERY WELL.
YOU HAVE TO COME BACK TO THE WOODS, BUNNY!
YOU HAVE TO.

WE WERE KING AND QUEEN FOR A WHILE AND EVERYTHING WAS GREAT, BUT THEN THIS BADGER BROUGHT THIS... THING. AND THE... THING... BROUGHT THE HUMANS AND THEN THE FIGHTING
BOO HOO HOO
BUT... I'VE SPENT SO LONG LOOKING FOR SOMEWHERE I FIT IN. I THOUGHT THAT WAS HERE.
SOB!
YEAH.
SKUNKY SAID YOU BELONGED HERE.

SKUNKY? HOW WOULD SKUNKY KNOW WHERE I BELONG?
C'MON, BUNNY. THINK IT THROUGH.
3...
2...
1...
GASP!
SKUNKY HAD SOMETHING TO DO WITH ME LEAVING HERE IN THE FIRST PLACE!
ATTABOY!
WHO'M I KIDDING, BEING IN THIS KENNEL IS DRIVING ME CRAZY! I NEED TO GET BACK TO THE WOODS!
YAYYYY!
TO KICK SKUNKY IN THE BUM!
GOOD LUCK, DUDE. HOPE YOU FIND THE ANSWERS YOU'VE BEEN LOOKING FOR.
RIGHT IN HIS BUM.
HEE HEE!
OKAY, THIS TIME I BROUGHT YOU... CARROTS...
OH FOR GOODNESS' SAKE, YOU'VE GONE AGAIN?!
BUNNY
JAMIE

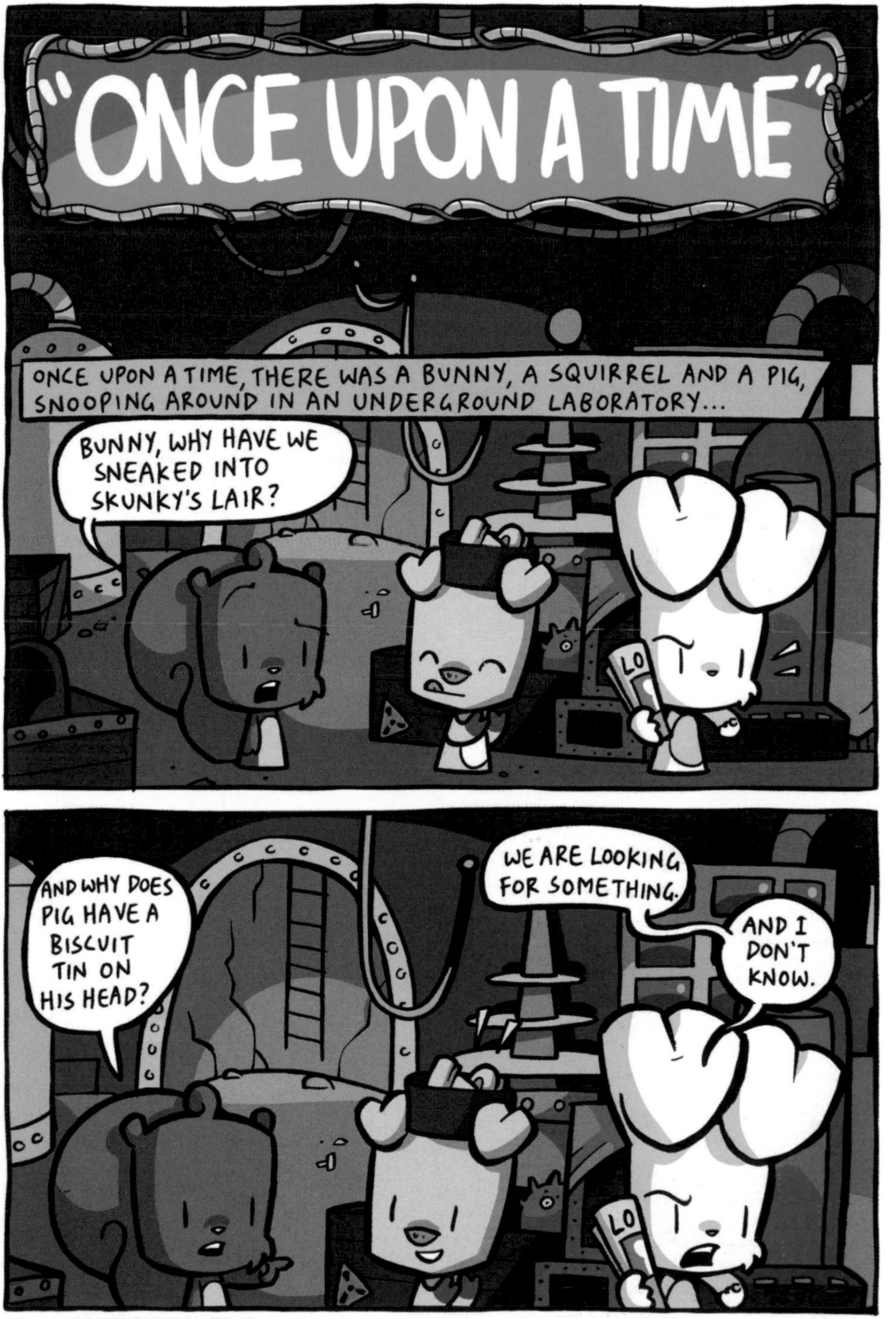

"ONCE UPON A TIME"

ONCE UPON A TIME, THERE WAS A BUNNY, A SQUIRREL AND A PIG, SNOOPING AROUND IN AN UNDERGROUND LABORATORY...

BUNNY, WHY HAVE WE SNEAKED INTO SKUNKY'S LAIR?

LO

A-HA! SKUNKY'S TIME MACHINE!
I KNEW IT'D BE HERE SOMEWHERE.
FWIP!
AND IT LOOKS LIKE HE'S UPGRADED IT SINCE HIS LAST HAPHAZARD EXPERIMENTS.
WE MIGHT HAVE A CHANCE.
SET DATE
SET TIME
VARIABLE
HEY! WHAT ARE YOU LOT DOING DOWN HERE?
EEK! GET IN!
SO LONG, SKUNKY! SEE YOU IN THE PAST!
BUT...
BWOOP!!!
BUT...
I'D MADE TEA.
BWOOP!
IT BROUGHT US BACK TO THE SAME PLACE! IT DIDN'T WORK!
IT'S THE SAME PLACE, BUT IT'S...

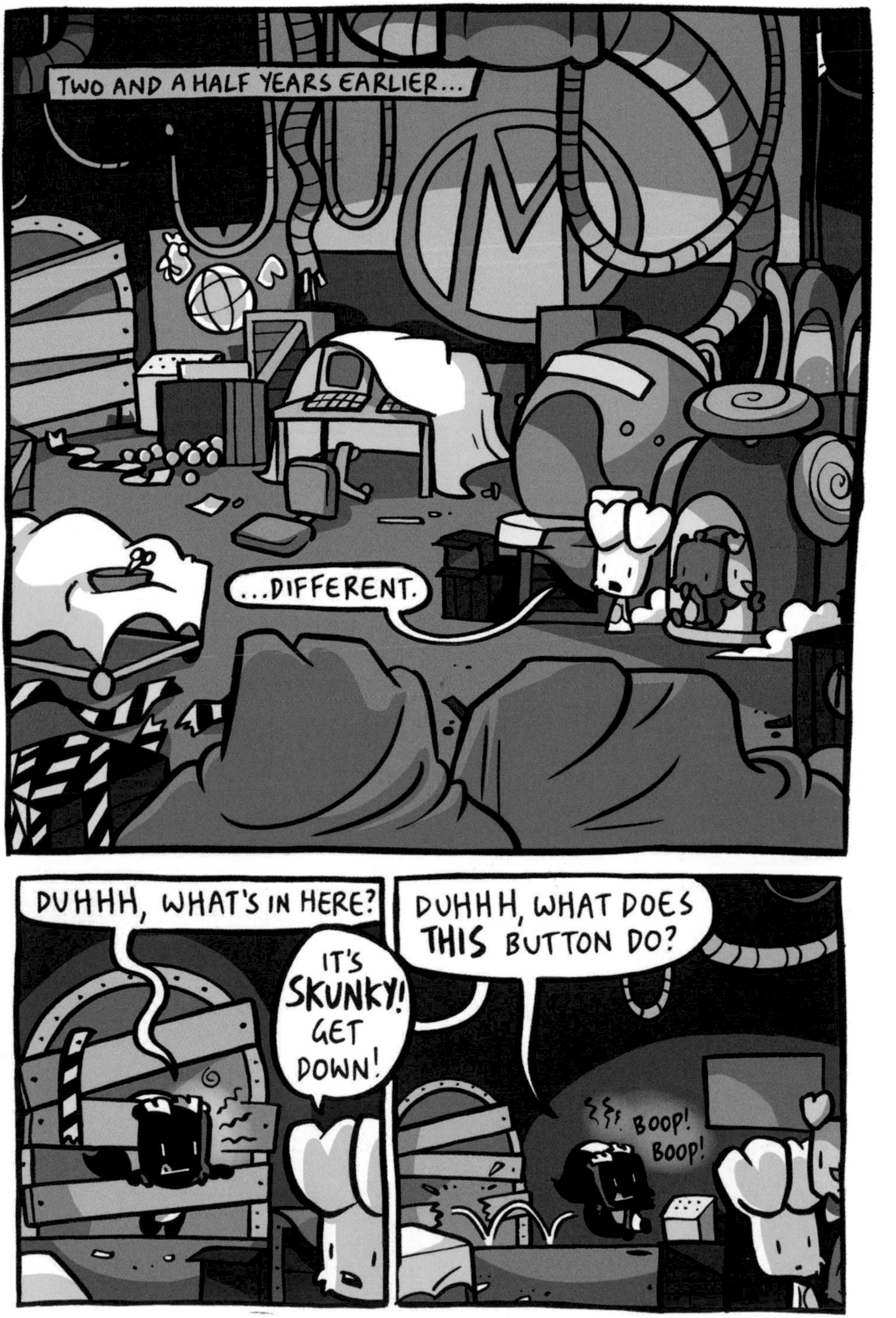

TWO AND A HALF YEARS EARLIER...

...DIFFERENT.

WHAT ABOUT THIS ONE?
BOOP! BOOP!
GASP! HE GOT EVEN SMARTER!
NO, PIG. HE SEEMS... STUPIDER.

WHAT DOES THAT SAY? DUHHH!
CLEVER-O-MATIC
AH WELL, IT'S SOMEWHERE TO SIT DOWN.

BZZZZZZ!
CLEVER-O-MATIC
DUHH...

RUMMMMMBLE!
IT'S OVERHEATING. IT'S GOING TO BLOW!
ATIC
WOULD ANYONE LIKE A BISCUIT?
NOT NOW, PIG.

ARGH!
EEP!
BONK!
CHOOM!!

I... AM... ...A GENIUS!!
SO, ALL THIS TIME, SKUNKY GOT HIS BRILLIANT BRAIN... FROM A MACHINE?!

HEY, BUDDY! I SAW WHAT JUST HAPPENED. THESE ARE MY WOODS, I FOUND THEM. I DON'T WANT NO SKUNKS TEARING THEM UP.

'FOUND' THEM? I'M A VASTLY SUPERIOR INTELLECT NOW, I COULD RULE THESE WOODS.

YOU CAN TRY IT, BUDDY, BUT I COME FROM THE CITY STREETS.
I KNOW HOW TO FIGHT.

OKAY, OKAY. LOOK, THERE'S NO REASON WHY WE CAN'T BOTH LIVE HERE, AS LONG AS YOU KEEP QUIET ABOUT WHAT YOU'VE SEEN TODAY.

AND WHAT DO I GET?

YOU GET THE GREATEST PRIZE OF ALL. TO INVENT YOURSELF! NO LONGER A COMMON STREET FOX, YOU CAN LIVE HERE AS WHATEVER CHARACTER YOU CHOOSE!
WELL, I'LL BE...

THE GUARDIAN OF THE WOODS!
MYSTERIOUS! BROODY!

AND I'LL BE FRENCH, TOO.
CLASSY, Y'KNOW. LIKE ZIS.

EXCELLENT! LE FOX, YOU KEEP OUT OF MY WAY, I'LL KEEP YOUR STORY, AND TOGETHER THESE WOODS WILL BE OURS.
BON!
THERE IS JUST ONE THING.

ZAT!
I, UH... I GOT OUT OF MY GARDEN.
I'M NOT SURE WHERE I AM.

HEE HEE! THAT BUNNY LOOKS LIKE YOU, BUNNY.
IT IS ME. TWO AND A HALF YEARS AGO!

LITTLE BUNNY, YOU DIDN'T SEE ME TRANSFORM FROM A STUPID IDIOT INTO A GENIUS DID YOU?
OR ME, ONCE A LOWLY FOX, NOW ZE GUARDIAN OF ZE WOODS!
UMM...NO?
GOOD!

LET'S JUST MAKE SURE, WITH THIS MEMORY RAY I PICKED UP IN THE LAB!
NO!
ZZZAP!!

WH...
WH...
WHAT HAPPENED?
DAZED!
NOTHING. NOTHING AT ALL.
FORGET EVERYTHING.
EEE! VISITORS!
I DON'T OFTEN GET VISITORS!

COME INSIDE! I'VE BEEN MAKING CARROT STEW! TONS OF IT!
BUNNY, THIS IS YOUR HOUSE NOW!
LET'S GIVE YOU A NEW IDENTITY SO YOU'LL NEVER REMEMBER!

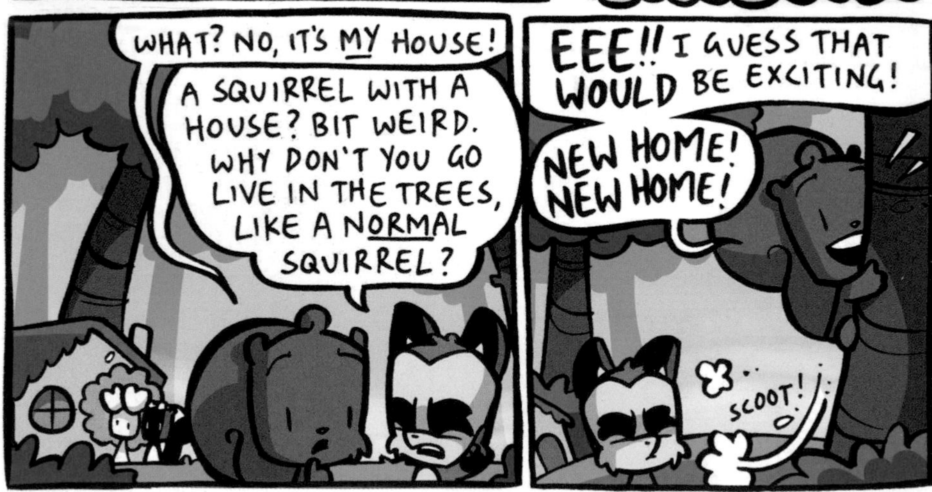
WHAT? NO, IT'S MY HOUSE!
A SQUIRREL WITH A HOUSE? BIT WEIRD. WHY DON'T YOU GO LIVE IN THE TREES, LIKE A NORMAL SQUIRREL?
EEE!! I GUESS THAT WOULD BE EXCITING!
NEW HOME! NEW HOME!
SCOOT!

I DON'T BELIEVE IT! SKUNKY WIPED MY BRAIN! HE INVENTED MY LIFE IN THE WOODS!
YOU'RE NOT GOING TO RUN AWAY AGAIN, ARE YOU, BUNNY?

NOT A CHANCE!
I NEED TO LEAVE THE CLUE THAT'LL LEAD ME TO WHERE I AM NOW.
I NEED TO COMPLETE THE LOOP!

SKUNKY, THERE'S A PIG OUT HERE TOO, NOW!
I HEARD A LOUD CHOOM!
I THOUGHT IT MIGHT BE SANTA.

IT'S FINE, I'LL USE MY MEMORY RAY AGAIN.

SHOO! GO ON, SHOO!
CLONK! CLONK!
OW!
OW!
OW!

BUNNY! IT'S ME, BUNNY. FROM THE FUTURE... WOW, WEENIE WAS MAKING A LOT OF CARROT STEW
I DON'T EVEN LIKE CARROTS.
I DON'T?
CARROTS
TAKE THIS. IT IS AN ADDRESS. KEEP IT SAFE AND ONE DAY IT WILL LEAD YOU TO THE TRUTH!
WHY CAN'T I REMEMBER ANYTHING?
LOST
BUNNY
RIP!
I MUST RETURN TO THE FUTURE NOW, BUNNY! BE PATIENT, AND YOU'LL BECOME ME!
ZZZ.
SURE.
WHAT?
SURE.
LET'S GO HOME.
BISCUIT?
GO ON, THEN.
BWOOP!!
ONCE UPON A TIME, THERE WAS A BUNNY, WHO WOKE UP ONE MORNING, UNAWARE HE HAD A WHOLE NEW LIFE AHEAD OF HIM...
YAWNN! WEIRD DREAMS.
...AND WHAT A VERY ODD LIFE IT WOULD BE.

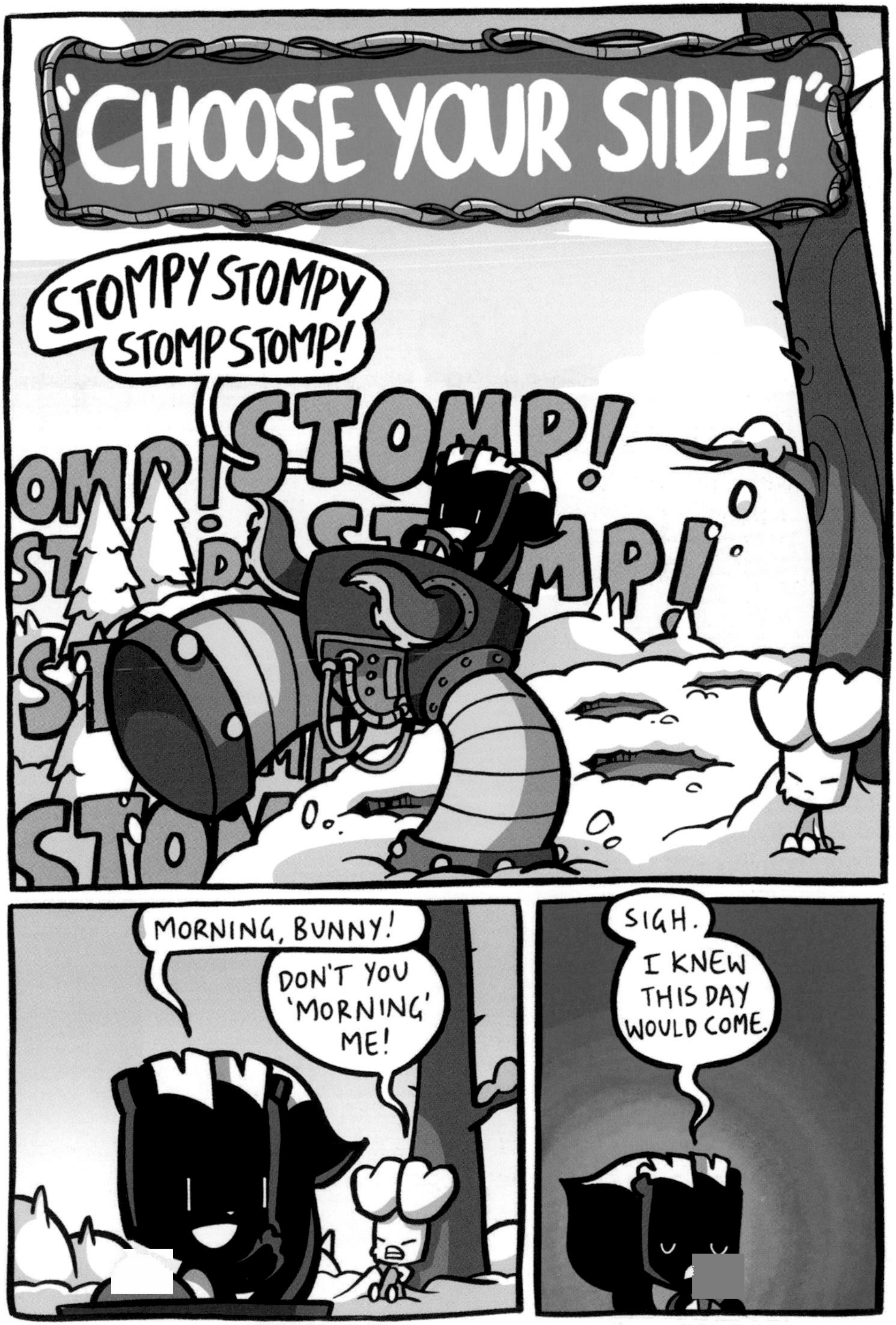

"CHOOSE YOUR SIDE!"

STOMPY STOMPY STOMP STOMP!

STOMP! STOMP!

YOU USED MY TIME MACHINE TO TRAVEL BACK TWO AND A HALF YEARS, AND SAW THAT I WIPED YOUR MEMORY, DIDN'T YOU?
YOU MADE ME THINK I LIVE IN THESE WOODS!

WELL, ISN'T IT NICE HERE? MAYBE YOU SHOULD BE THANKING ME!
STOP IT, EVIL!!

NO LONGER SHALL YOU DESTROY THESE WOODS! NOT WHILE WE, THE...
RATHER GOOD SQUAD
...ARE HERE! WITH ITS HEROES...

SASSY PIG!

FEISTY SQUIRREL!

GRUMPY FOX!
I DIDN'T WANT TO BE INVOLVED IN THIS.

WHAT ARE YOU DOING? WHY ARE YOU ATTACKING MY STOMP-O-MATIC!
KICK! KICK!
WE ARE THE GOOD GUYS! WE THWART EVIL!
YOU ARE BEING EVIL!

I WASN'T! I WAS JUST STOMPING AROUND! I HAVEN'T DESTROYED ANYTHING YET TODAY!
HUFF!
KICK IT!

WHAT ABOUT YOU, 'LE' FOX? YOU NOT JOINING IN?
THEN AGAIN, WHICH SIDE WOULD YOU TAKE?
GERROFF!

BECAUSE ON THE ONE HAND, YOU'VE HELPED US PROTECT THE WOODS OVER THE YEARS, LIKE A GOOD GUY WOULD...

BUT THEN ON THE OTHER, YOU DID MAKE A PACT WITH SKUNKY TO KEEP EACH OTHER'S SECRETS.

AND YOU'RE NOT EVEN FRENCH!
GASP!
GASP!
GASP! HOW DID YOU KNOW?
BZZT!
ARGH! YOU LITTLE ROTTERS!
YOU'VE KICKED THE STOMP-O-MATIC TOO HARD! IT'S SHORT CIRCUITING!
STOMP! STOMP! STOM
I CAN'T CONTROL IT! I'M...
...DESTROYING EVERYTHING!
STOMP! STOMP! STOMP

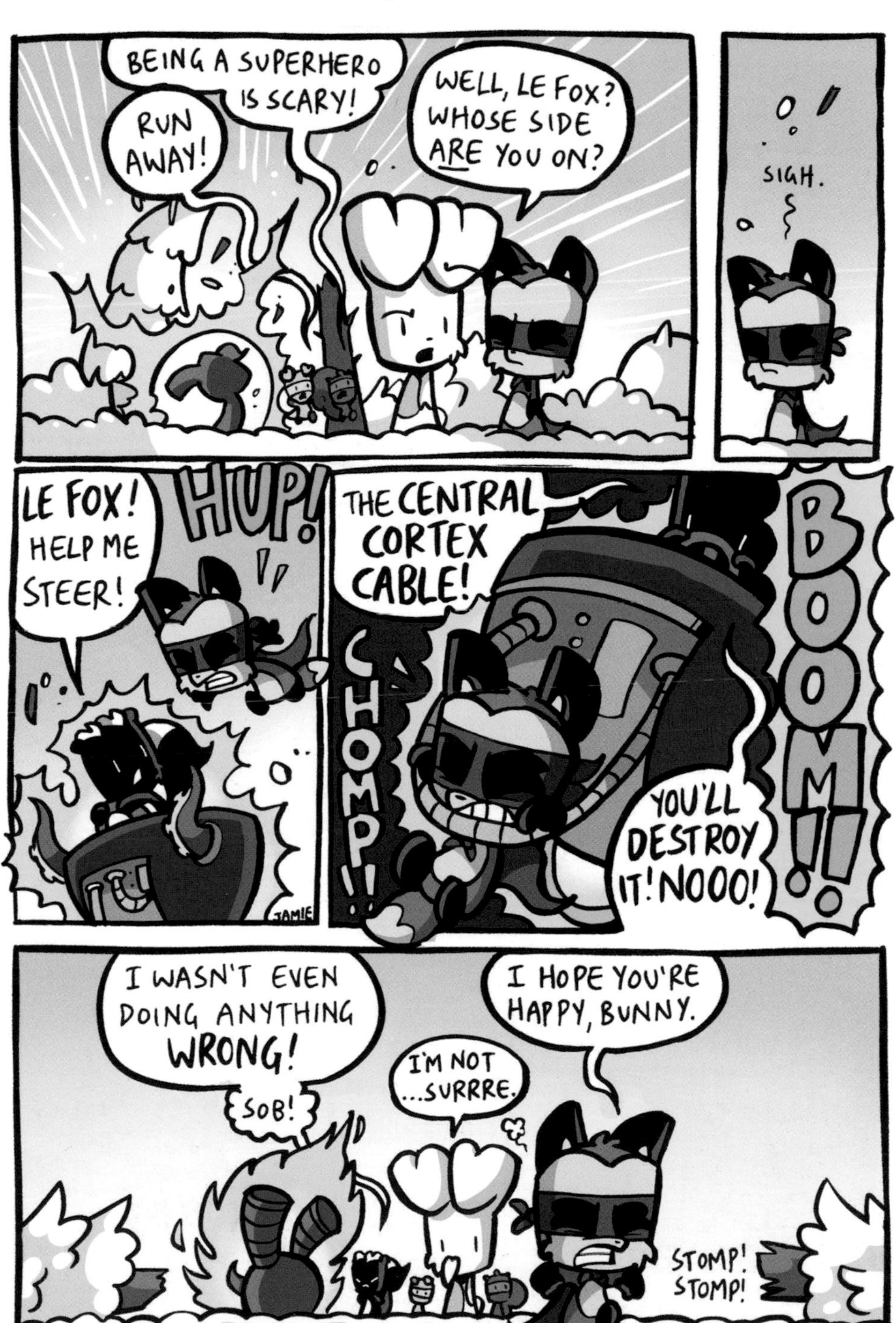
BEING A SUPERHERO IS SCARY!
RUN AWAY!
WELL, LE FOX? WHOSE SIDE ARE YOU ON?
SIGH.
LE FOX! HELP ME STEER!
HUP!
THE CENTRAL CORTEX CABLE!
CHOMP!!
YOU'LL DESTROY IT! NOOO!
BOOOM!!
JAMIE
I WASN'T EVEN DOING ANYTHING WRONG!
SOB!
I'M NOT ...SURRRE.
I HOPE YOU'RE HAPPY, BUNNY.
STOMP! STOMP!

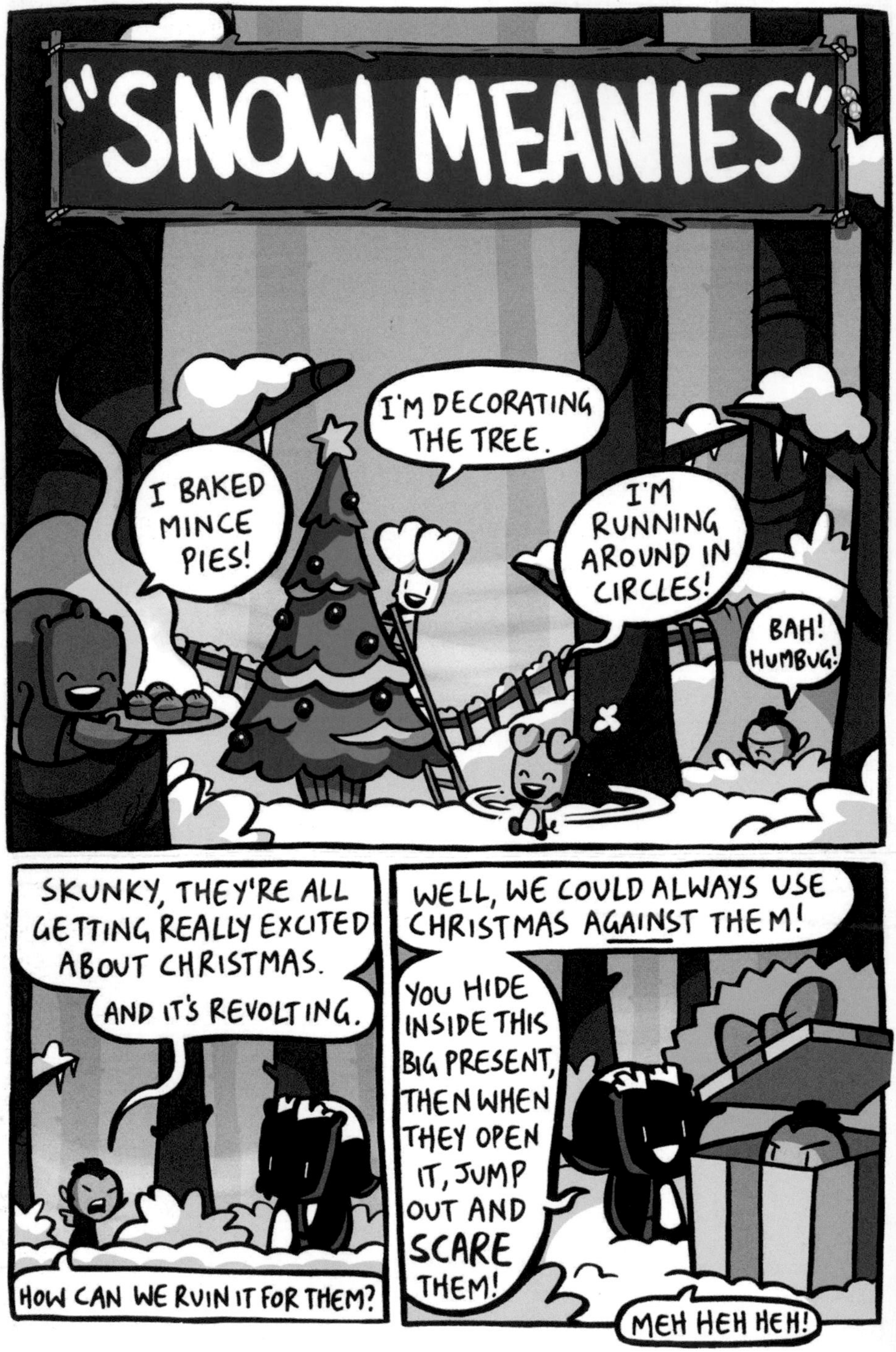

"SNOW MEANIES"

I BAKED MINCE PIES!
I'M DECORATING THE TREE.
I'M RUNNING AROUND IN CIRCLES!
BAH! HUMBUG!

OOH LOOK, A PRESENT!
IS IT FOR US?
HEH HEH!

YOU CAN'T OPEN IT YET. CHRISTMAS DAY ISN'T FOR AGES!
AWW.
OKAY.

ZZZZZ...

YET ANOTHER FAILED PLAN, SKUNKY. THEY DIDN'T EVEN COME CLOSE.
AND THEN I FELL ASLEEP.
IT WAS JUST A DECOY, TO KEEP YOU OUT OF MY WAY WHILE I INVENT...

THE...
SNOW MEANIES!
GRUARGH!
#☆!!
THEY'RE ACTUALLY ROBOTS, COVERED IN SNOW, PRIMED TO DESTROY!
GLEEE!
GRUUU!
HAR HAR, BRILLIANT! THEY'RE DESTROYING EVERYTHING!

THEY'RE EATING MY MINCE PIES! **THEY'RE EATING MY MINCE PIES!**
CHOMP! CHOMP! CHOMP!

AW. THEY WERE FRESH OUT OF THE OVEN, TOO.
HISSSS!!
WHAT? NO!

YOUR DELICIOUS HOT BAKED TREATS HAVE **MELTED** MY SNOW MEANIES!
OOPS.
SORRY!
GLOOP!

ACTUALLY, WITHOUT THEIR SNOW, THEY LOOK KINDA...
...TERRIFYING.

YAYYY! MY MINCE PIES SAVED CHRISTMAS!
CLANK! CLANK! CLANK!
SCREEAM!!
WHAT A CONFUSING FEW MINUTES THIS HAS BEEN.

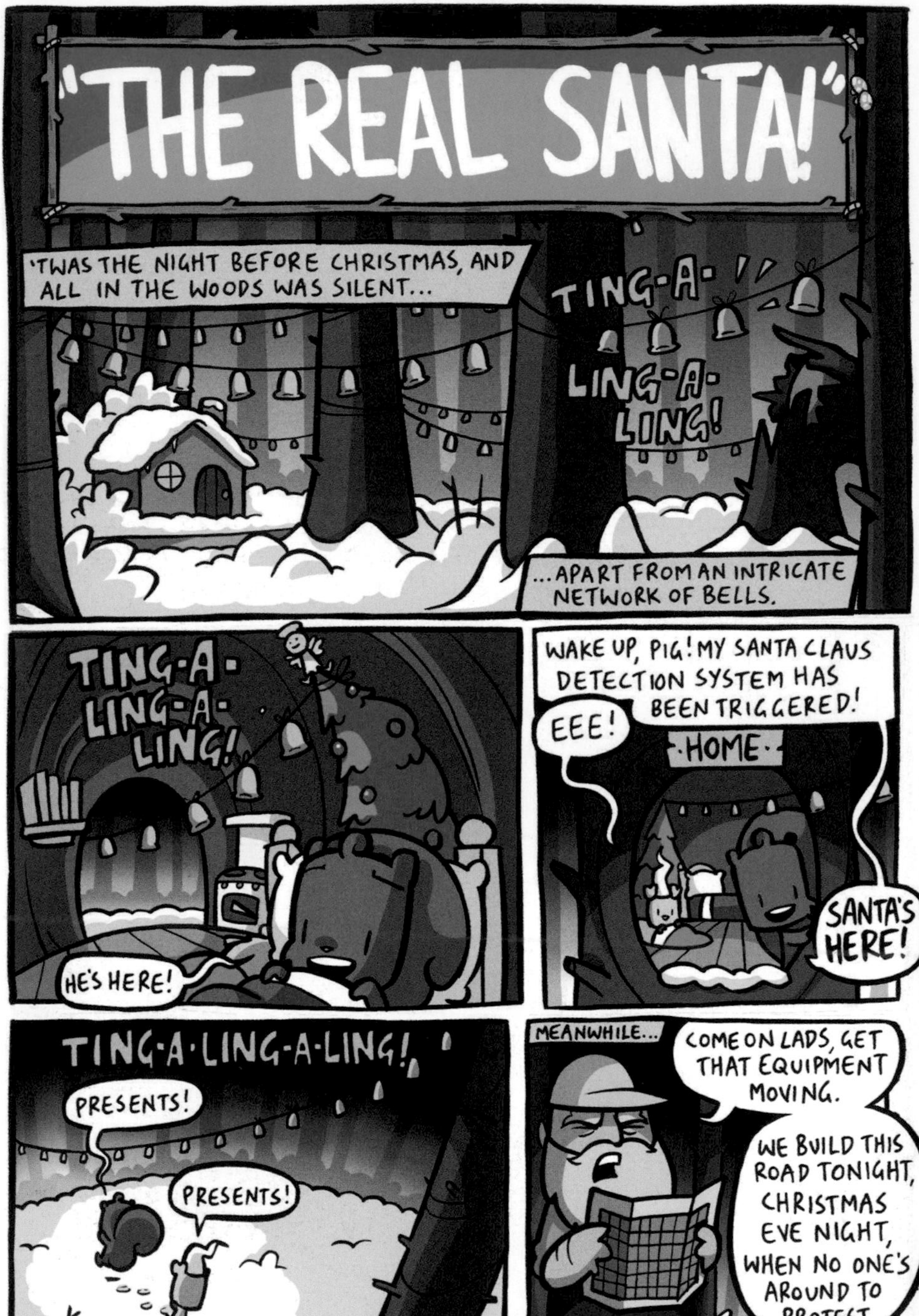

"THE REAL SANTA!"

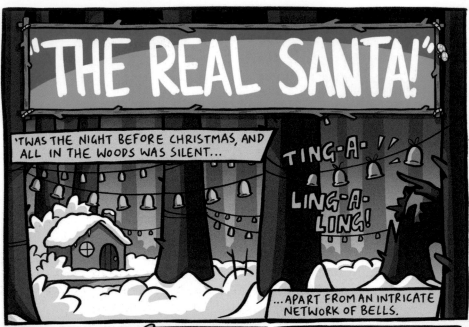

'TWAS THE NIGHT BEFORE CHRISTMAS, AND ALL IN THE WOODS WAS SILENT...

TING-A-LING-A-LING!

...APART FROM AN INTRICATE NETWORK OF BELLS.

TING-A-LING-A-LING!
HE'S HERE!

WAKE UP, PIG! MY SANTA CLAUS DETECTION SYSTEM HAS BEEN TRIGGERED!
EEE!
·HOME·
SANTA'S HERE!

TING-A-LING-A-LING!
PRESENTS!
PRESENTS!

MEANWHILE...
COME ON LADS, GET THAT EQUIPMENT MOVING.
WE BUILD THIS ROAD TONIGHT, CHRISTMAS EVE NIGHT, WHEN NO ONE'S AROUND TO PROTEST.

I'VE BROUGHT THE TOOLBAG, FOREMAN!
GOOD. SIGH! WHAT ARE THESE FLIPPING BELLS I KEEP WALKING INTO?
TOOLS
TING-A-LING!

ARE YOU SURE HE'S SANTA? HE SWEARS A LOT, FOR SANTA.

HE'S FAT AND HE HAS A BEARD, JUST LIKE SANTA.
OH, HE IS SANTA!

THAT'S NOT SANTA. HE LOOKS MORE LIKE ONE OF THE HUMANS WHO WANT TO BUILD THEIR ROAD RIGHT THROUGH OUR WOODS!
WHY WOULD SANTA DO THAT?

OUT OF ZE WAY!!
?

I AM LE FOX, GUARDIAN OF ZE WOODS!
THEIR METAL AND CONCRETE MUST PASS THROUGH ME BEFORE ANY ROAD IS BUILT!

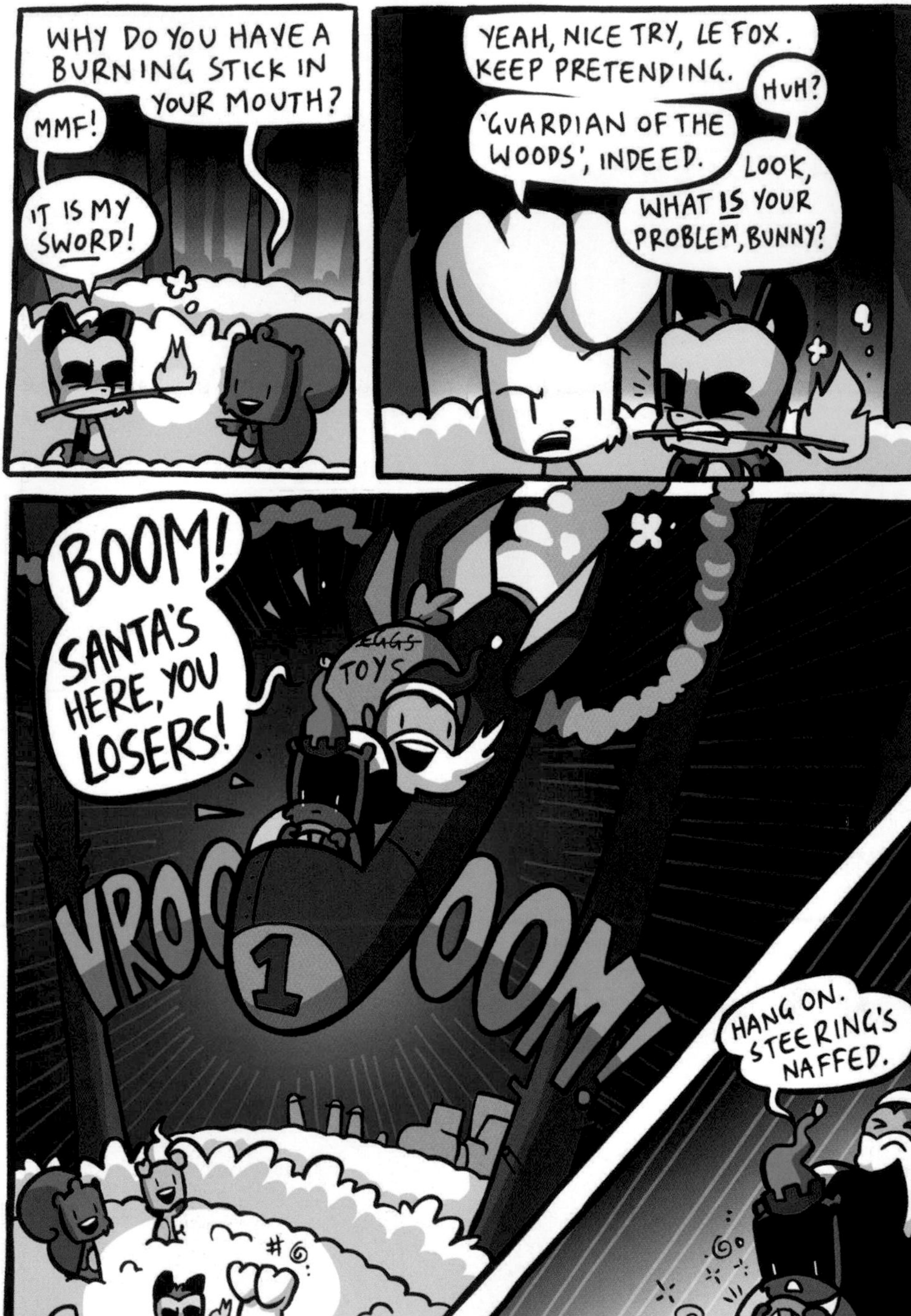

BOOM! SANTA'S HERE, YOU LOSERS!

~~EGGS~~ TOYS

VROOOOOM!

1

HANG ON. STEERING'S NAFFED.

CRASH!!
GAH! BAD! BAD ELF SKUNKY! HOW AM I SUPPOSED TO DELIVER THE 'PRESENTS' NOW?!
YOU'RE NOT SANTA, YOU'RE MONKEY.
AND WHY'S SKUNKY AN ELF?
UM...
SHH, BOYS AND GIRLS.
YEAH, WHY AM I THE ELF? I'M THE GENIUS HERE, AND YOU'VE DRESSED ME UP LIKE AN IDIOT!
SHHH! YOU'RE BLOWING OUR COVER!

WE ARE SUPPOSED TO BE FLYING OVER THE WOODS DROPPING A BAG FULL OF WHIFFY EGGS ON EVERYONE.
Y'KNOW, FOR CHRISTMAS.
EGGS TOYS
PONG!
BUT WE CAN'T EVEN GET THAT RIGHT!

YOU DO BETTER, THEN. I'M SICK OF BEING YOUR DOGSBODY!
C'MON, LE FOX! WHY DON'T YOU FINALLY TELL EVERYONE THE TRUTH?
#!!
#!
NON!

HEY, WHAT'S GOING ON HERE?

BUILDING A ROAD THROUGH THE WOODS.
TONIGHT? BUT IT'S...
...IT'S CHRISTMAS EVE!
YOU CAN'T!

I'M THE RANGER OF THESE WOODS. YOU HAVE NO AUTHORITY HERE.
NO? I DO HAVE A BUNCH OF FIVES, THOUGH.

!!

THIS ISN'T THE CHRISTMAS SPIRIT AT ALL. EVERYONE'S FIGHTING!
PRESENTS WOULD CHEER THEM UP!

WHAT DID SANTA BRING IN HIS SACK?
THESE TOYS ARE RUBBISH!
TOOLS

ARE YOU KIDDING? THESE TOYS ARE BRILLIANT!
SANTA BROUGHT ME ALL I ASKED FOR!
HUG!

YOU'RE SUPPOSED TO BE SANTA!
OH! OH, YES. HO HO HO! LET'S SEE WHAT PRESENTS I BROUGHT YOU THEN!

MEH HEH HEH! A FESTIVE STINKY-EGG ASSAULT!

A... ACTION BEAVER? WHAT ARE YOU DOING IN THERE?
EGGS
TOYS
UH OH...

ARE YOU ALL RIGHT? YOU DON'T LOOK WELL.
HE GOT INSIDE THE BAG! HE **ATE** THE WHIFFY EGGS!
RUMMMMMMMMBLE!
RUN AWAY!
RUN AWAY!
~~EGGS~~ TOYS
HUUUP!!
BURRRRPP!!
EURGH! SMELLS LIKE WE HIT A MAJOR GAS PIPE!
PACK UP, LADS. WE CAN'T BUILD A ROAD HERE.
AW.

EVERYONE, EVACUATE!
BOO HOO! IT'S STINGING MY EYES!
HO HO HO! HERE I AM, THE REAL SANTA CLAUS...
GROSS! EGGY PUMPS!!
BLEURGH!!
BRUMM!
I THINK WE'RE OKAY, EVERYONE! I THINK THE WOODS ARE SAVED!
MERRY CHRISTMAS TO US ALL!
EVEN LE FOX.
I NEED A CAREER CHANGE.
YUM!
JUST WHAT I WANTED!
HMPH.
BZZT!
A STRING OF BELLS!

"DOOR B"

WE FOUND A THING!
A THING!
ANOTHER THING?
BUT WE ALREADY HAVE PLENTY OF THINGS.

NOT LIKE THIS THING! WE WERE EXPLORING THE OTHER SIDE OF THE WOODS AND WE FOUND...
...A BUILDING!
...A TEMPLE!
...A BEMPLE!

COME AND SEE, BUNNY!
DO I HAVE TO?
WE LEFT A TRAIL OF CROUTONS TO FIND OUR WAY BACK!
!
HM. I DO LIKE CROUTONS.

RIGHT! COINCIDENTALLY, AND COMPLETELY UNRELATED TO WHAT THEY'RE DOING, I'VE DECIDED TO GO. GOODBYE!
SKUNKY? WHERE ARE YOU GOING?

I'VE HAD IT WITH THESE WOODS, AND EVERYONE IN IT. I DESERVE FAR BETTER.

SKUNKY! STOP!
YOU WON'T KEEP ME HERE, MONKEY.

NO, IT'S JUST I WENT TOILET SOMEWHERE AROUND THERE.
BECAREFUL WHERE YOU TREAD.
RRGH!

AND I AM ESPECIALLY SICK OF MONKEY! EVERYONE TREATS HIM LIKE THE DEVIL OF THESE WOODS, BUT LOOK AT HIM! HE'S AN IDIOT!
HOI!
HE HAS A POINT, MONKEY.

WHEREAS I AM THE GENIUS AMONGST US, AND I GET IGNORED!
WELL, NO MORE!

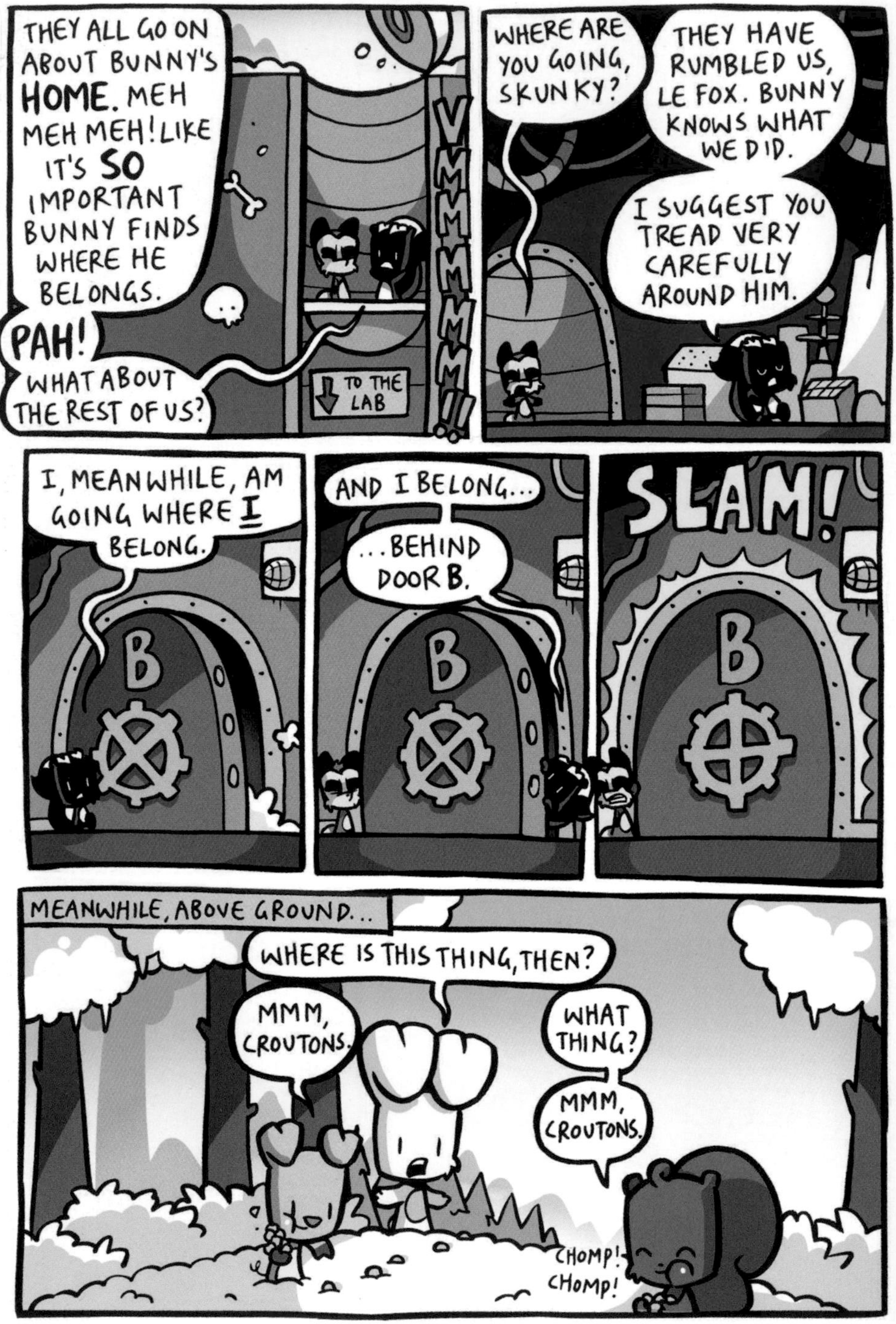

THEY ALL GO ON ABOUT BUNNY'S **HOME**. MEH MEH MEH! LIKE IT'S **SO** IMPORTANT BUNNY FINDS WHERE HE BELONGS.

PAH!

WHAT ABOUT THE REST OF US?

TO THE LAB

VMMMMMMM!!

WHERE ARE YOU GOING, SKUNKY?

THEY HAVE RUMBLED US, LE FOX. BUNNY KNOWS WHAT WE DID.

I SUGGEST YOU TREAD VERY CAREFULLY AROUND HIM.

I, MEANWHILE, AM GOING WHERE I BELONG.

AND I BELONG...

...BEHIND DOOR **B**.

SLAM!

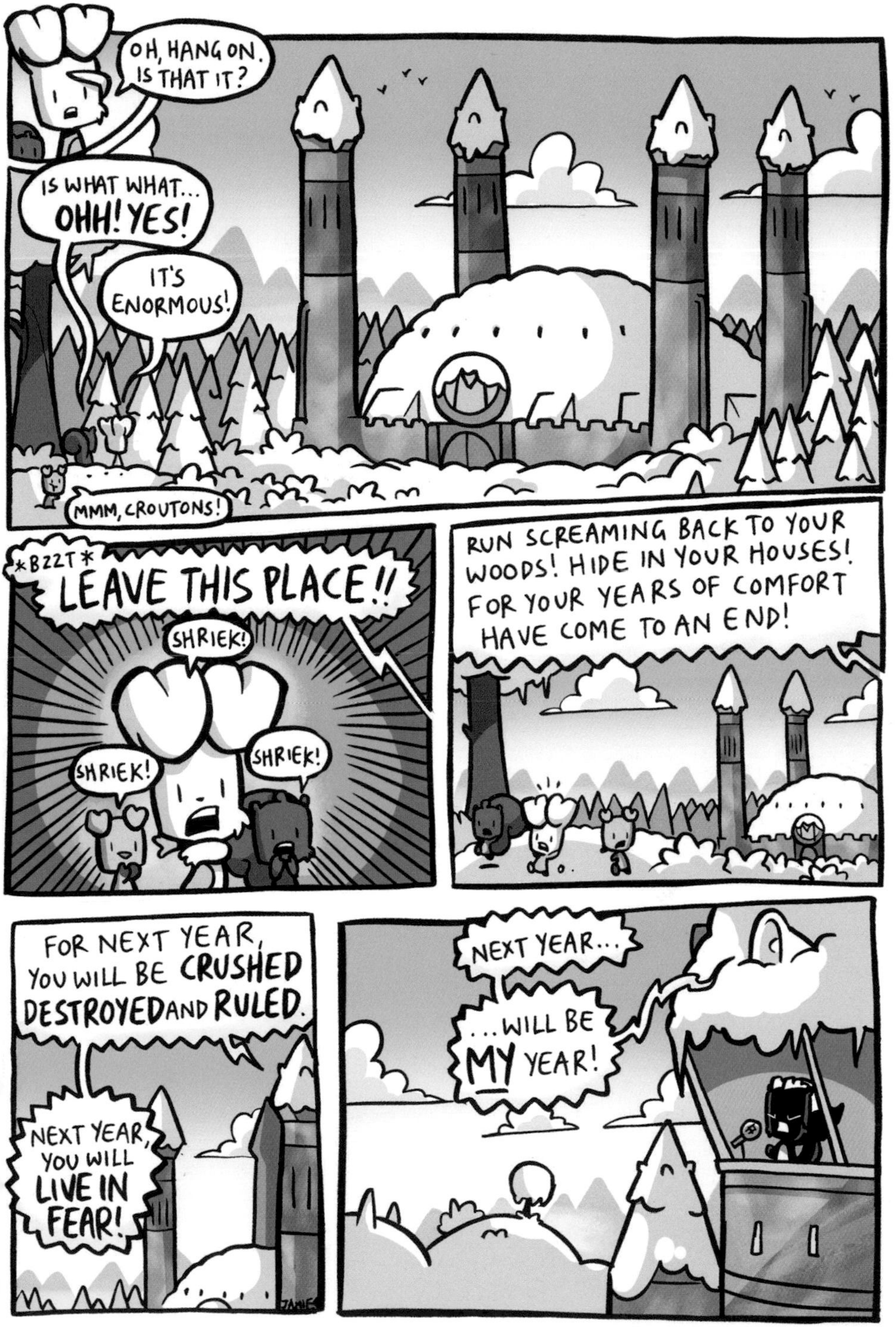

OH, HANG ON. IS THAT IT?
IS WHAT WHAT... OHH! YES!
IT'S ENORMOUS!
MMM, CROUTONS!

THE END!

TO BE CONTINUED IN...
BUNNY VS MONKEY
AND THE LEAGUE OF DOOM!

HOW TO DRAW PIG

1

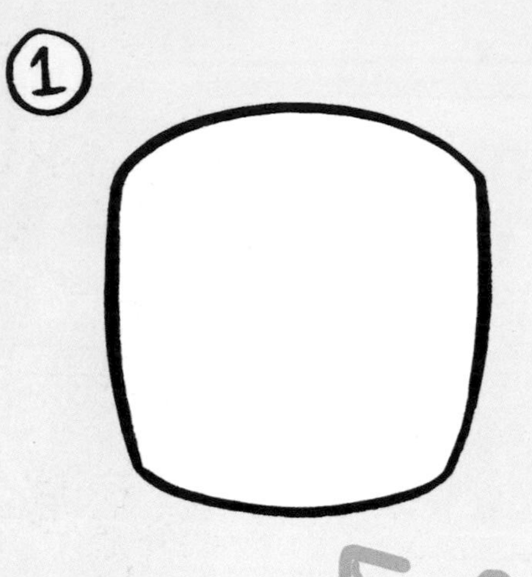

FIRST, LET'S DRAW **PIG'S HEAD!** A LOT OF THE CHARACTERS IN BUNNY VS MONKEY HAVE THE SAME SHAPE OF HEAD– A **BULGING SQUARE!**

2

IF YOU'VE READ BOOK 1, YOU'LL KNOW HOW WE DRAW BUNNY'S EARS. **PIG'S EARS** LOOK VERY SIMILAR, BUT THEY'RE SMALLER, AND MORE SPACED APART.

NOW WE DRAW PIG'S FACE!

TO WORK OUT WHERE PIG IS LOOKING, TRY USING A PENCIL TO DRAW A CROSS ON HIS HEAD...

...THIS HELPS US WORK OUT WHERE TO PLACE HIS **EYES**!

DON'T FORGET PIG'S EYEBROWS!

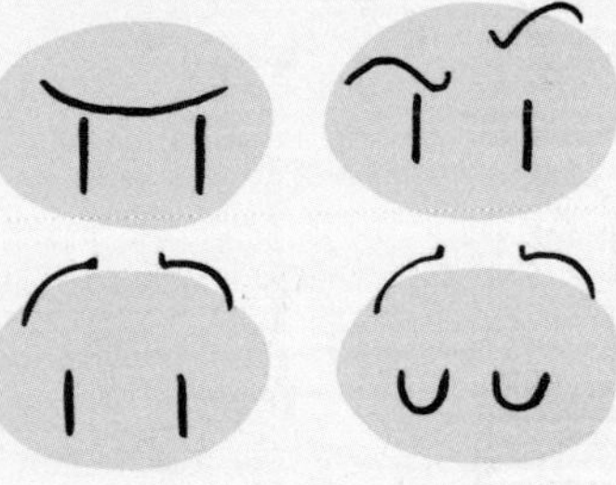

MOVE THEM UP AND DOWN TO FIND DIFFERENT EXPRESSIONS!

PIG'S **NOSE** IS A TRIANGLE WITH TWO DOTS INSIDE IT.

AND LASTLY, ADD A LITTLE **SMILE**!

NOW LET'S DRAW PIG'S BODY!
1
TO WORK OUT HOW TALL PIG IS, DRAW A LINE FOR THE GROUND.
PIG'S BODY IS A CURVED LUMP!
2
DON'T FORGET THE CIRCLE ON PIG'S BELLY!
3
FOR PIG'S ARMS, TRY DRAWING CURVED SAUSAGES
4
ADD A THUMB AND TWO FINGERS.
5
THEN DRAW IN PIG'S TWIRLY TAIL!
WHY NOT TRY DRAWING PIG IN LOADS OF DIFFERENT POSES, WITH DIFFERENT FACIAL EXPRESSIONS? HAVE FUN WITH HIM!

HOW TO DRAW SKUNKY

SKUNKY'S HEAD IS THE SAME SHAPE AS PIG'S HEAD!

SKUNKY'S EARS ARE LIKE TINY LITTLE BOBBLES EITHER SIDE OF HIS HEAD.

AND THEN WE DRAW TWO ROWS OF SPIKED WHITE FUR BETWEEN THEM!

LET'S DRAW SKUNKY WITH A DEVIOUS EXPRESSION...

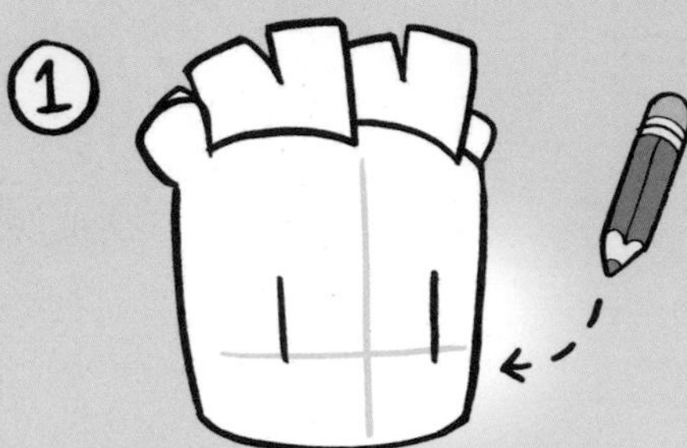

FIRST, PENCIL IN THE CROSS SO WE CAN SEE WHERE SKUNKY'S **EYES** WILL GO...

...AND LET'S ADD SOME MEAN-LOOKING **EYEBROWS** ABOVE THEM!

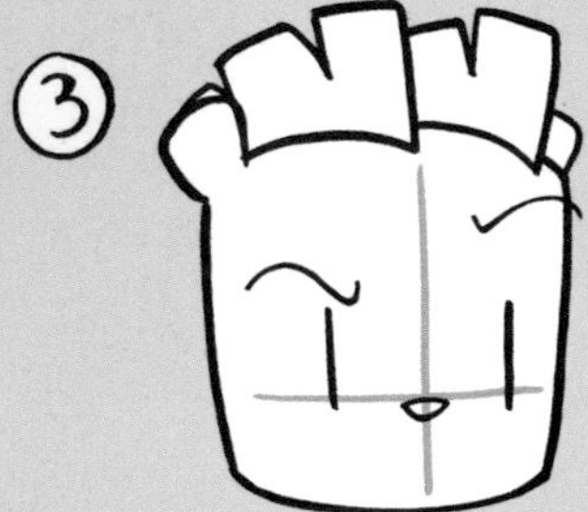

SKUNKY'S **NOSE** IS JUST A TINY LITTLE TRIANGLE.

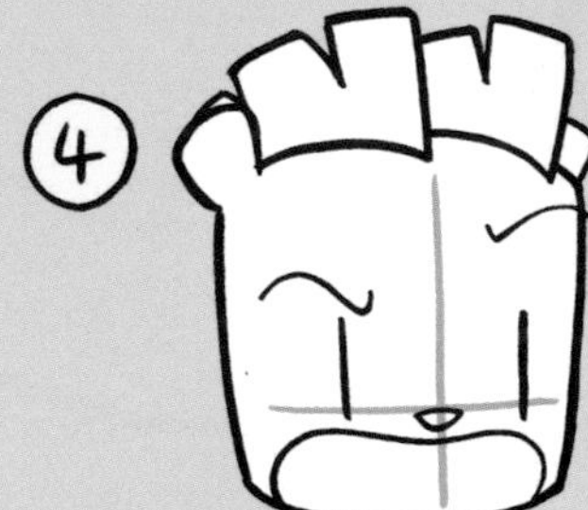

WE WANT HIM TO HAVE A GREAT BIG MISCHIEVOUS GRIN - SO LET'S DRAW HIS **MOUTH** AS BIG AS WE CAN...

WE DON'T NEED TO DRAW EACH AND EVERY ONE OF HIS TEETH - JUST A WAVY LINE TO SHOW THEY'RE CLENCHED TOGETHER!

AND LASTLY, SKUNKY HAS A LITTLE TUFT OF **CHEEK HAIR!**

FINALLY... SKUNKY'S BODY!

... BUT SKUNKY WEARS A **LAB COAT**, SO BE SURE TO DRAW IN THE NECK AND BUTTONS!

SKUNKY'S BODY IS THE SAME **LUMP** WE DREW FOR PIG...

4

LET'S GIVE SKUNKY ONE ARM BY HIS SIDE, AND ONE ARM POINTING AS IF HE'S JUST HAD AN **EVIL IDEA**!

AND FINALLY, SKUNKY'S **BIG BUSHY TAIL**! IT TUCKS IN BEHIND HIM!

AND THERE YOU GO, WE'VE DRAWN **SKUNKY**! NOW COME UP WITH SOME CRAZY INVENTIONS FOR HIM TO BE PLAYING AROUND WITH!

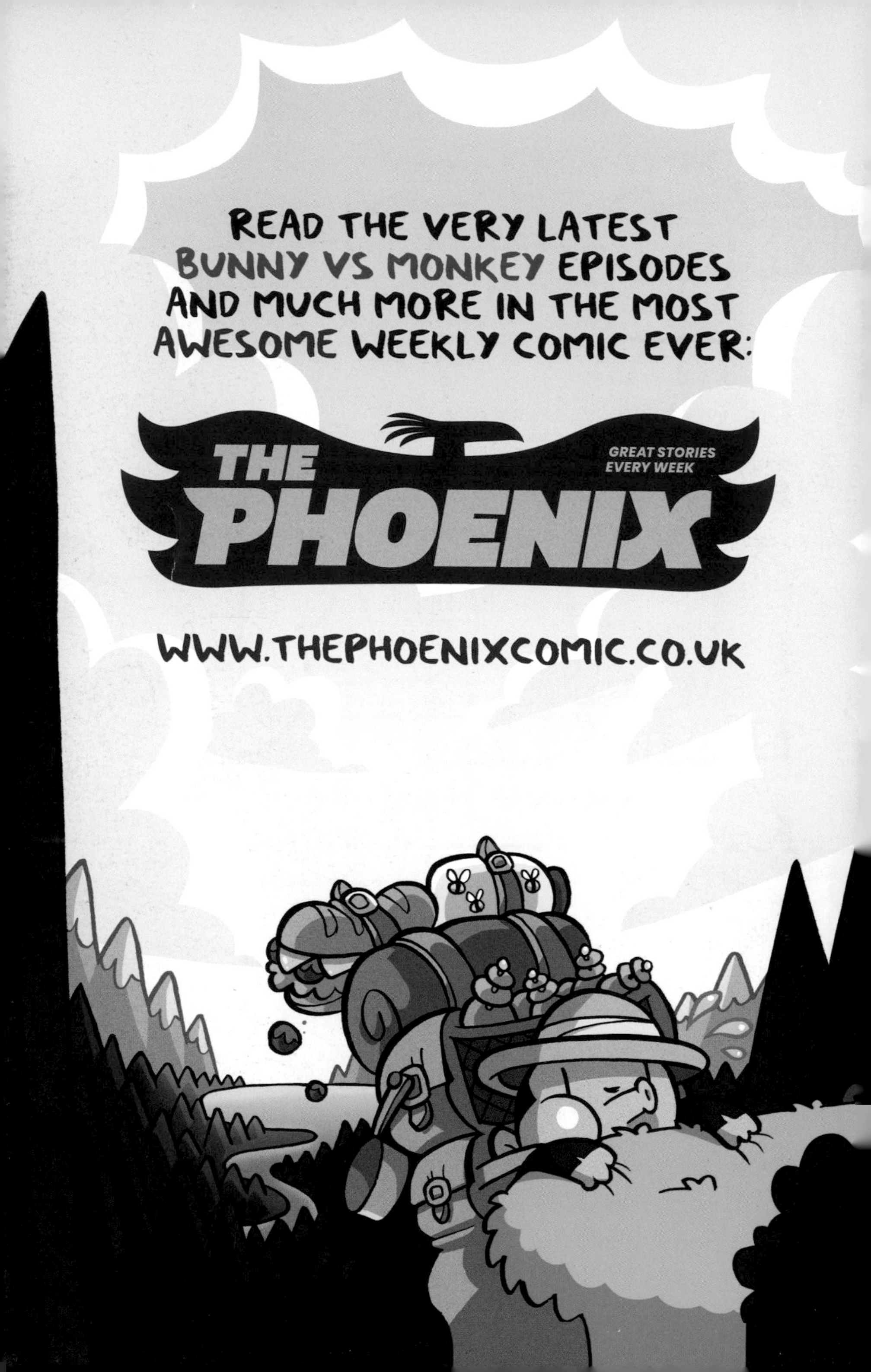

EW YEAR, NEW LOOK, SAME GREAT STORIES!
THE PHOENIX
GREAT STORIES EVERY WEEK
ONK ONKK!
LEGACY
A brand-new chapter
GOREBRAH!
Happy St Bodgekin's day!
GET INTO SOME TROUBLE WITH EDEN'S GREATEST INVENTOR!
CATCH UP ON THE EPIC LEGACY STORY SO FAR!
THE PHOENIX
GREAT STORIES EVERY WEEK
I HATE PIXIES
Do you love frogs? We do!
STAR COMIC!
WINNER AND RUNNERS-UP ANNOUNCED THIS WEEK!
BLANCMANGE IS IN YOUR FUTURE...
THE PHOENIX
GREAT STORIES EVERY WEEK
HEY! THAT'S MY HOUSE!
I HATE PIXIES
You may now kiss the bride!
CORPSE TALK
The power of Pytheas!
PLUS ALL THIS:
Claire: Justice Ninja, Book Club, The Smalls, Big News, Inkspot Challenge, Squid Bits, Ministry of Mistakes, Susie and Brad & more!

JAMIE SMART'S
BUNNY VS MONKEY
THE FUNNIEST FIGH
EVER HAS BEGUN
JAMIE SMART'S BUNNY VS MONKEY
OUT NOW!

DISCOVER THESE OTHER HILARIOUS BUNNY VS MONKEY BOOKS!

ENTER THE WORLD OF JAMIE SMART

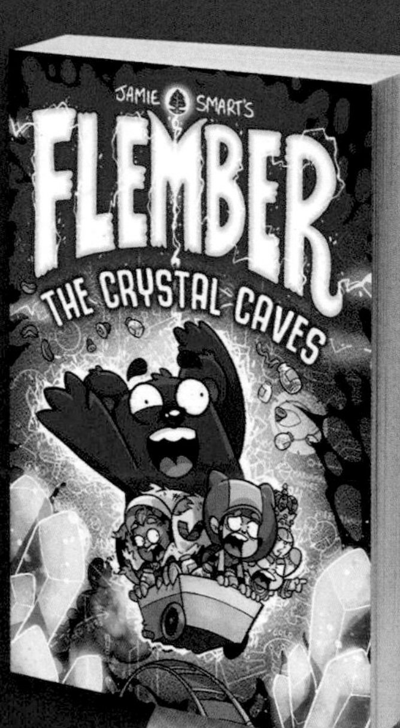

DISCOVER THE MAGICAL POWER OF FLEMBER, WITH BOY-INVENTOR DEV, AND HIS BEST FRIEND BOJA THE BEAR!

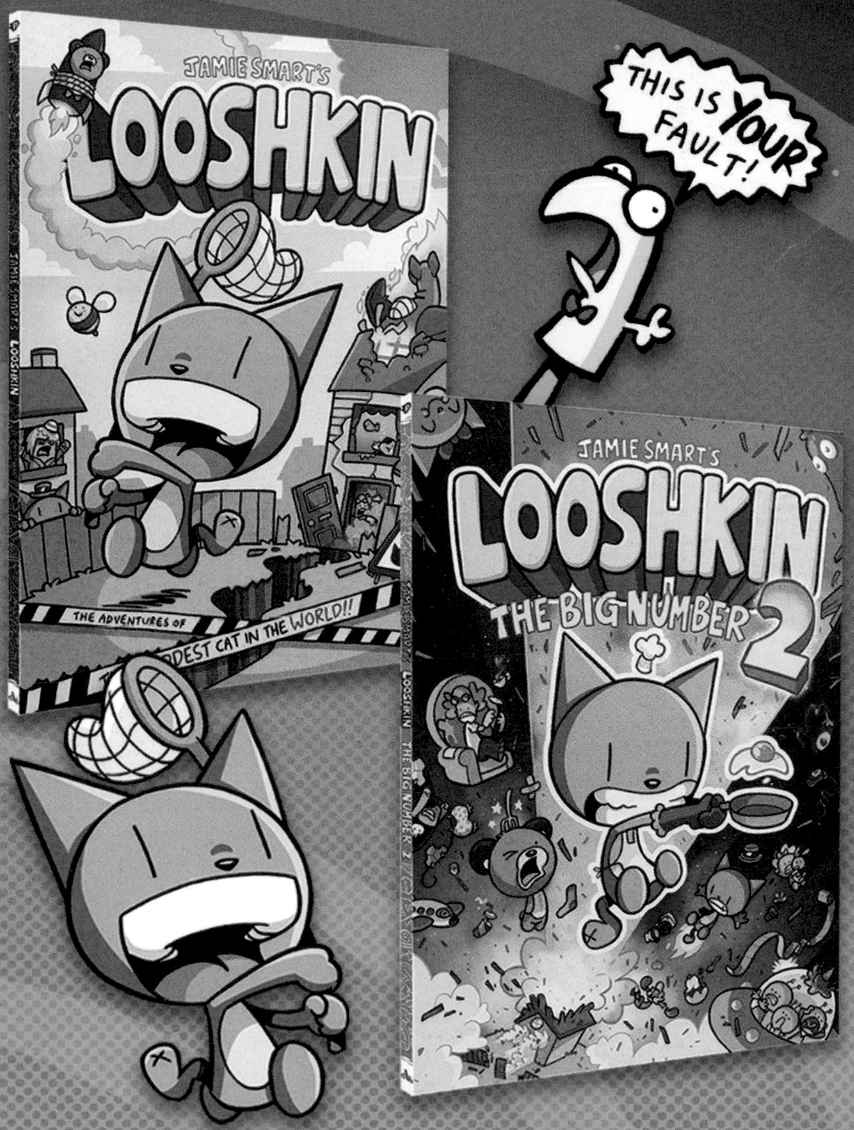
JAMIE SMART'S
LOOSHKIN
THE ADVENTURES OF
DDEST CAT IN THE WORLD!!
THIS IS YOUR FAULT!
JAMIE SMART'S
LOOSHKIN
THE BIG NUMBER 2

JAMIE SMART HAS BEEN CREATING CHILDREN'S COMICS FOR MANY YEARS, WITH POPULAR TITLES INCLUDING *BUNNY VS MONKEY*, *LOOSHKIN* AND *FISH-HEAD STEVE*, WHICH BECAME THE FIRST WORK OF ITS KIND TO BE SHORTLISTED FOR THE ROALD DAHL FUNNY PRIZE.

THE FIRST TWO BOOKS IN HIS *FLEMBER* SERIES OF ILLUSTRATED NOVELS ARE AVAILABLE NOW. HE ALSO WORKS ON MULTIMEDIA PROJECTS LIKE *FIND CHAFFY*.

JAMIE LIVES IN THE SOUTH-EAST OF ENGLAND, WHERE HE SPENDS HIS TIME THINKING UP STORIES AND GETTING LOST ON DOG WALKS.